To Kelly

With best wishes.

Robert B.Chambliss, MD.

THE FOLLOWING BOOK

IS WRITTEN FOR

MY CHILDREN AND GRANDCHILDREN,

AND YOURS

FOR THOUGHTFUL CONSIDERATION

Acknowledgements

Like the immortal words of the poet Tennyson, I believe " I am a part of all I have met." God has put some incredible people in my life, most of them from Breckinridge County. Each of them has become a part of my total person. I think Tennyson also meant that I have become a small part of the lives of all those I have touched. I am grateful to God for this opportunity to be a part of their lives – hopefully, a positive influence.

Most of all, I thank God for the opportunity to have practiced medicine in Breckinridge County for more than forty-eight years. I give Him total credit for any success I may have had.

I want to thank the good people of Breckinridge County who have honored their native son by their trust and support. I have had a very enjoyable and satisfying medical practice among my own people for whom I have great love.

I am eternally grateful for a dedicated and loving wife who has been an equal partner in my medical career and I give her credit for our accomplishments. She encouraged me to write this book, (as have many of my patients) and has been patient and supportive.

A special thanks to Linda Holloway, my secretary and office manager for almost fifty years, who never complained about the hundreds of hours we spent with the manuscript. She is a special friend.

I thank my pastor, the Reverend Dr. Paul Gibson, who led me to Susan Graham, a noted editor and teacher from Fort Mill, South Carolina, who helped me organize the book. Many thanks to Barbara Miller, a local high school teacher, for doing a thorough review of the grammar punctuation, and spelling, which are not my forte.

The book is filled with "thank yous" for my staff, colleagues, family, hospital personnel, and all the loyal patients that include five generations. I have enjoyed every minute of my service to the people of Breckinridge County who have treated me the best.

LOVE IS THE THEME

You will notice a common theme that runs through this book.

A love for my parents, who got me started off on the right foot.

A love affair with my wife, who has been an equal partner in the success of our family and in my medical practice.

A love for my boys and a lifelong commitment to them.

A love for the practice of medicine.

A love for my patients and staff and an effort to treat them like family.

A love for agriculture and farming.

A love for my community and its good people.

A love and appreciation for our country.

A Kentucky boy's love for basketball.

And, most important, a love for God and a deep faith in His promises.

LOVE IS SUPREME

"Life's a Trial and Life's a Worry," a poem by Dr. Charles Jarvis, used with permission of Pam Jarvis Foster.

"Darnell, Chambliss Reign Over Greeks." Used with permission of The Kentucky Kernel, University of Kentucky.

"Build Me a Son," a poem by General Douglas MacArthur, Used with permission of the General Douglas MacArthur Foundation

"Bryan Chambliss Sets Conference Record." Used with permission of Breckenridge Herald News.

"Country Doctor, an Autobiography." Used with permission of Breckenridge Herald News.

"Brain Injury Opened Door to Life of Art." Used with permission of Louisville Courier Journal.

"Greatly Blessed, Highly Favored" by Larry Gatlin and William J. Gaither. Used with permission of Mike Curb Music, Hannah Street Music and Barton Music.

Jim Chambliss bungy jump photo. Used with permission of A. J.Hackett Bungy, New Zealand.

Painting of Breckenridge High School and Elementary School. Used with permission of the artist Becky Taul.

Ariel Photo Of Chambliss Farm. Used with permission of Donn K. Wimmer, Clarion Publishing Company.

Various Photographs of Family Members taken by Olin Mills Studios. Each used with permission of Life Touch, Inc.

Photograph of rafting trip. Used

Table of Contents

Bobby Chambliss
3rd Grade
Breckinridge County Elementary School

CHAPTER 1

The Beginning

Where do you begin to tell the story of becoming a country doctor? Let's start with a nine-year-old third-grader whose picture tells it all. Does this picture depict a child who has the confidence to become whatever he should choose to become? In retrospect, I think it does.

At the time, I had never thought about what I might do. I was happy on the farm, the eighth of nine surviving children of Paul and Elmina Chambliss of Hardinsburg, Kentucky, loved and adored by seven older siblings and a younger sister–secure and happy, and certain that all was right in the world. Every day was a new adventure of learning and discovery. I lived in the precious present and thought very little of the future.

What I did know for certain is that I wanted to be a basketball player in the image of my hero, Ralph Beard – three time All-American and a member of the University of Kentucky Fabulous Five, who was also born and lived in Hardinsburg, Kentucky until his parents took his talents to Male High School in Louisville.

I lived with a basketball in my hands day and night until it became a part of me. My only dream was to be a player for the University of Kentucky. Thousands of other Kentucky boys, I am confident, had this same aspiration. You see, basketball in Kentucky is our second religion and binds us together into the Big Blue Nation. You go to basketball heaven and then to God's heaven, in that order.

I was born December 19, 1937, on a Sunday morning in the Chambliss farmhouse, which was located near the Hardinsburg city limits. It was snowing, with some accumulation. It was one of the few times that my mother missed teaching her Sunday school class at the Hardinsburg Baptist Church. She delivered easily, at home, unassisted, and our family doctor, Dr. John E. Kincheloe, who delivered over 7,000 babies in his career, got there in time to tie and cut the umbilical cord. Both of these exceptional people would greatly influence my life.

I was born poor in earthly possessions, but rich in family, rock-solid rural social traditions, and teachings of a Christ-centered, loving, caring, serving, evangelical church. I was also taught a work ethic that almost guarantees success. I grieve when I think of how much America has changed in two generations and how much harder it is for my children to prepare their children for life and harder yet it will be for my great- grandchildren to prepare their children for life.

I was reared on a rural Kentucky farm surrounded by people who loved me, feeling secure, nurtured by my parents' wisdom, pampered by my loving and admiring sisters, challenged and toughened up by my father and brothers, and taught how to be a good neighbor by the good neighbors who lived in our rural community. It was much later in life that I realized God had placed me here, blessed me, and cultivated in my heart a desire to please Him and a desire not to disappoint Him. I did a little of both in time, but I have carried the teachings and influence of my childhood with me all the days of my life, and they have served me well.

I thank God often for this early training and have tried to pass it on to my three sons and others. I am gratified to see them pass it on to their children. This is ever so much harder to do now in this world of rapidly changing moral values, political correctness, and abandonment of Godly principles and God's commandments which we have traditionally depended on to guide our paths starting with the wisdom of the early founding fathers of our country, the greatest Constitution ever written, and reliance on the Bible, God's Holy Word to lead and guide us.

We were just a few years out of the Great Depression. That spring, Breckinridge County experienced the Great Flood, with the Ohio River at our northern border rising to unprecedented heights, forcing many of our citizens from their homes.

The Chambliss family experienced its own disaster in the winter of 1937 when our barn caught fire from some overheated fodder, destroying the barn and silo and all its contents, which included the corn fodder, hay, grain, horses, and all the cattle.

It was customary back then to put all the livestock in the barn on cold winter nights and lock them in. This is no longer practiced, since farmers have learned that cattle can take care of themselves and survive outside in any kind of weather, with proper nutrition and water.

This loss was particularly devastating for my parents, who had just survived the Great Depression of the 1930s with seven children. They had lost their first farm in 1930 to a bank failure and bankruptcy, and were just getting a new farming operation underway. I remember my mother saying that on that very afternoon they were out in the pasture admiring the herd of Hereford cattle they had built up and remarking how blessed they were. They never questioned why it happened. Their faith in God never depended on current circumstances. They vowed to survive this, too, just as they had survived the Depression, but they continued on with intense memories of the Depression.

One heartwarming story I will remember forever. School was soon to start in September, and my mom and dad had six school-age children. They had gone barefooted all summer long, but with school approaching, my mother was agonizing because they had no shoes decent enough to wear to school.

My father had a brother who had a farm at the Hardinsburg city limits adjacent to ours. When my parents lost their farm to bankruptcy in the Depression, he offered to help them buy the adjacent farm, and they farmed together. His brother was a bachelor and somewhat of a recluse. In spite of antisocial behaviors, he had a heart of gold, and although he didn't go to church with us, I learned that he was a decent, fair, honest, solid citizen who was "different," as Mom would acknowledge. While we were taking communion at church, he would stay at home, sitting in the swing on the front porch, sipping a little bourbon – preferring to be alone.

When he heard the kids had no shoes to wear to school, he thought about how he could help. He had one milk cow but didn't drink much milk (preferring bourbon). He took his only milk cow to the market and sold her and took the money and gave it to my mother and said, "Go get those kids some shoes," and then quickly walked away.

My mother cried as she received this unexpected gift. I suspect this is why Uncle Vernon made a quick exit. Despite his "peculiarities," my mother loved and appreciated him dearly and would never let anyone say anything negative about him. She even named her ninth child Ruth Vernon. She got the kids shoes, and they never missed a day of school. Most of them were nearly straight-A students.

It takes more than shoes to get the kids ready for school, but Mom took care of the rest. She made all our clothes--even underwear, which we called BVD's. I don't know what BVD stands for! I know they make you itch! Eventually, after the Depression, they started selling livestock feed in 100-pound bags of calico and colored material instead of burlap. Mom kept the whole family in feed sack clothes she made on an old treadle (foot- operated) Singer sewing machine, which she kept running far into the night along with pre-paring for the next day's meals, giving baths, and reading her well-worn Bible. She then put my younger sister and me to bed. The last thing she would do at the end of each day was kneel at the couch in the living room and pray for her family, naming each of us individu-ally and our needs. I remember standing behind the door at times, listening to every word. What an impact this left on this impression-able child. I still tear up when I think of it and often when I was about to do something bad. Did I do bad things? Of course, just like all God's children whom He created in His image, which includes the freedom to choose. We all make bad choices in life – but it sure helps to have a praying mother to turn us around (sometimes with a switch).

There are many Great Depression stories I remember. But, of course, everyone in Breckinridge County was all in the same boat, and they all worked through it together.

Elmina Lyons Chambliss
Dr. Chambliss' mother as a teenager

CHAPTER 2

My Mother

On my thirty-fifth birthday I received a birthday card, as always with a letter or a poem from my mother. She began, "Dearest, Bob, thirty-five years ago today the last thing in the world we needed was another baby boy." And then the letter got more sentimental as she shared with me how unique I was and what I meant to her.

She loved each of her eleven children dearly, including the one she lost as an infant and the other as a three-year-old toddler who died prematurely within twenty-four hours after contracting diphtheria. This little girl was a child prodigy who could read from the *Louisville Courier-Journal* at age three. My mother talked of her often.

My mother treated me and each of my brothers and sisters as an only child – meeting our special needs, since we were all different. Someone asked her which one she loved the most. She said, "I will answer like the mother of Charles Wesley, early leader of the Methodist church, when she was asked the same thing about her nineteen children. "I love the one who is sick until he is well. I love the one who is lost until he comes home."

Mom had the reputation of being a Bible scholar equal to a seminary professor. She was self-taught and continued to teach until the age of eighty-six. She not only knew the Bible but followed its teachings and was more like Jesus than anyone I have ever known. Legend has it that my mother taught her Sunday school class the following Sunday after I was born, with me sound asleep in a rocking cradle on the floor and Mom sitting at the classroom table with one foot rocking the cradle to make sure that I didn't disturb the class.

My family seldom said, "Under the circumstances, what would Jesus say or do?" but rather, "What would Mom Chambliss say or do?" Her influence was felt by her very large family and the people of Hardinsburg and Breckinridge County. Although her activities confined her life to a small Kentucky farm, her influence has been felt around the world by her progeny and others who carry her influence with them to the farthest points of the world, like the Galilean who never traveled very far from Nazareth but changed the entire world with a three-year ministry.

She was the oldest of a large rural family of very modest means. Always a brilliant student, she had to "board" in town to go to high school. After her sophomore year, her father told her he couldn't afford to send her any more. My mother was not to be denied. In 1915, all you had to do to be a teacher was pass a teacher's examination, which every teacher took each year. Mamaw, as we affectionately called her, took the test and not only passed but made the top score in the county, beating all of her former teachers and the superintendent of schools. So, she became a teacher and continued her education in this way. She had a burning desire to attain a college education, but she married and taught school so my father could attend college at Clemson.

Then there were eleven children and twenty-four grandchildren, and the college education that she wanted so much came through each of them, one by one. With each college and professional degree, each Phi Beta Kappa, each valedictory honor, each Summa Cum

Laude, there was Mamaw in the background, realizing her impossible dream.

She loved life, she loved God, and she loved people. Her entire life was devoted to others, and I never heard her mention any problem of her own. Every day was a challenge. She worked harder than anyone around her. She studied and learned every day of her life. Always intensely competitive, she was interested and conversant in sports, religion, politics, community affairs, and world affairs until the day she died. She touched everyone who came in contact with her, and everyone who knew her was a better person for the experience. She died within twelve miles of where she was born and never ventured too far away from the farmhouse where she spent her life, but her influence has spread around the world through those she touched. You see, early in life she decided she would be in it all the way, 110%. Each of us has within us the power to make that same decision. She influenced my life more than any other person in the world. She always listened when I wanted to talk. She talked only when she sensed I was in the mood to listen. She was never as subtle as she tried so hard to be – she wrote me "special letters on special occasions" and sometimes even poems to gently remind me about my "purpose in life." I loved her with all my heart.

Here is a poem she wrote me when we moved from our house next door into our "dream house on the hill" behind their house in the center of the farm:

These are some of my thoughts on the night of
the day you moved up on the hill, February 1, 1980.

So long we looked across the way
To a house that was lively, full and bright.
We watched it together. We loved what we saw.
But now all is changed – it's as dark as night.

I think there is nothing quite so sad
As a house that is empty, silent and dark,
Unless it's a life devoid of dreams,
No plans – no light – not even a spark.

It was never so with you, I know,
For you have always had your dreams.
You set your goals, you marked your chart,
And worked so hard, but with joy, it seems.

Tonight I am happy for you and yours
In your beautiful house up on the hill,
And knowing there's love to make it a home
Makes me even happier still.

Having this dream of yours come true
Must bring a feeling of joy and pride.
I feel it, too, and I know full well
That God's part in it can't be denied.

He has blessed you well, for a purpose, I think,
With a body strong and a will to succeed,
With a loving heart and willing hands,
And eyes to see so many in need.

So it doesn't matter where you live,
Up on the hill or down by the road.
The needs are still there – your task is, too,
To try to lighten another's load.

This is what life is all about.
It's better far than fortune or fame,

To know – to love – to feel the hurt,
And to be able to help in His dear name.

So, I sit here tonight with a grateful heart
For who you are and what you have done,
And I offer a prayer for you and yours
That you'll know life at its best, all the
 years to come.
Congratulations, best wishes and love always,
 "Mom"

On December 20, 1985, my mother died. She was a young eighty-eight years old. In her hospital room she was watching the University of Kentucky – East Carolina basketball game with several members of her family. The score was 24-22. She had just commented that Kentucky would have to play better if they expected to pull this one out. She had earlier said it just didn't look right without Coach Joe B. Hall on the bench. Before the game she had watched *Wheel of Fortune* and solved all the phrases quicker than anyone in the room. Earlier she had played a game of Scrabble and won. No one could beat Mamaw, as my sons called her, at Scrabble.

No one could beat Mamaw at the game of life because she was "in it" all the way, with all the intensity and enthusiasm she could muster – even at the end with her frail body and failing heart. For eighty-eight years she was a positive force and guiding light, not only for her family to which she was devoted, but to her church, her community, and her country.

My mother was my hero. Fortunately, before she died I had the opportunity to tell her that she was. Her motto was:

Good, better, best
Never let it rest
Until the good becomes better
And the better becomes best.

I consider myself fortunate to have been born her fourth son and tenth child in that cold, airy farmhouse on that snowy December Sunday morning almost seventy-nine years ago.

For a child who aspired to be a country doctor, what better start could you get? I remember President Lincoln's words about his mother: "All I am or all I ever hope to be I owe to my darling mother."

Paul Bryan Chambliss
Senior, Clemson Agriculture College, 1919

CHAPTER 3

My Father

AN HONEST DAY'S WORK

If I learned one thing from my father, it was that he gave every day his best shot. Not just on Mondays or during the harvest season when three weeks' work had to be done in one week; not just when someone was watching or when he was challenged by a younger worker, as he often was — but every day of his life. Whether he was shucking corn, cutting tobacco, or working on the Farm Bureau membership drive, my father led the pack and seldom was bested in anything he undertook. He led by example and never asked a hired hand or a son to do anything he didn't do himself. I know now it was mostly out of necessity, but he seemed to get great satisfaction from what he called "an honest day's work."

He was one of eight children, and his father, a schoolteacher and farmer, died at age forty-nine of tuberculosis when my father was only five years old. The year was 1902.

His mother, left with the responsibility of a large farm family, assumed the role of head of the family and breadwinner. She and her children, by hard work, dedication, and faith, made it through the hard times. Not only did they make it – the children excelled. Four daughters became schoolteachers. The oldest son graduated from Clemson College and went on to become President of the Montana Power and Water Company. My father, also a graduate of Clemson College, was a successful farmer and merchant. He worked his way through Clemson, which, at that time, offered degrees in agriculture and engineering. My father opted for electrical engineering because he said, with a twinkle in his eye, "The better students at Clemson took engineering."

The work ethic, learned as a child out of necessity, stayed with him all the days of his life and he was a classic example of "hard work not killing you" – living to age eighty-four, raising nine children, and leaving a modest estate to show for his labors.

Dad was my role model, my mentor, and from the start I tried my best to emulate him. Whatever the work of the day, I entered into it with enthusiasm, intent on outworking everyone in the field.

We were cattle and Kentucky burley tobacco farmers. I took pride in the fact that I could hoe tobacco faster or cut (harvest) tobacco faster or pitch more hay than anyone in the neighborhood. This carried over into the classroom and sports and became as much a part of my life as it had my father's. When I was an intern at the Louisville General Hospital, I was the recipient of the George P. Caldwell Proficiency Award given annually to the outstanding young intern. I did not win the award because I was the most brilliant intern but because I was the most willing to do the hard work (thirty-six hours on and twelve hours off for twelve months).

My wife has often chided me for being a workaholic, but by the truest definition of a workaholic, I do not qualify. I admit being a hard worker and probably a hard taskmaster – but, like my father, I have tried to live and lead by example.

I think it sounds better to be called an "extra effort person," so named by Dr. Hugh Riordan, a Wichita psychiatrist, who heads up the Olive W. Garvey Center for the Improvement of Human Functioning. I do very much believe in giving every day its best shot whether it be at work, at play, at church, or on vacation.

Dad's "Honest Day's Work" philosophy has definitely been instilled in me. Dad taught by example. My philosophy developed from watching his example and listening to his every word.

Dad taught me that everyone on this earth should be able and willing to work with his or her hands. You should not be afraid to get them dirty. No matter how successful you are or plan to become, you should never think it beneath you to dig in the earth, sweep a floor, or clean out a barn stall.

You should also be willing to start out at the most menial job and as the lowest man on the totem pole. He taught that winners work at doing things that the majority of the population are not willing to do. Your future success will be determined by how you perform at these jobs.

If you are working for minimum wage frying hamburgers at McDonalds or at Winn-Dixie stocking shelves, give it your best. Be the best hamburger fryer or the best stock boy you can be. Be on time, work hard, work through breaks or stay late if you must, and always be loyal to your employer. Try to increase your efficiency, get along with your fellow employees, meet the public well, and look for ways to increase your employer's bottom line. Always be ready to assume new responsibility and give the extra effort. Always be thinking as you work "Isn't there some way this job can be done easier, quicker, better?" Read everything you can get your hands on about your job or your service or your product.

Why? What's in it for you? A successful career is in it for you! Someone is going to take notice. It may not be your present employer, but if you give an honest day's work, someone is going to notice and give you a raise or a better job. It may be another employer – but someone will – because hardworking, enthusiastic workers are in demand. Dad taught that hustling nearly always guarantees your present job and will earn you raises and promotions in the future. Don't just do what you are paid to do, but go the extra mile.

The work habits you develop early will be the work habits that will stay with you the rest of your career. Hopefully you will find work that you enjoy – because the more you enjoy it, the more success you usually have. There will be times in everyone's life when you must do work that is boring and disagreeable. But let me be quick to remind you that this is the case in even the most glamorous occupations and professions. You simply have to discipline yourself to do this kind of work at all levels. An actor or athlete who performs to the applause of millions has spent hundreds of hours in boring and sometimes agonizing preparation. So let me advise you to look at your sometimes boring and disagreeable minimum-wage work as preparation for more rewarding work in the future.

Now don't get me wrong, work alone won't make you successful. You have to have the right vehicle, and you have to have a dream. You wouldn't travel coast to coast on a tricycle. Your dream will usually lead you to the right vehicle to get you where you want to go. In addition to this you need knowledge, skills, and imagination. You need to base your life on truth, integrity, and honesty. But all of these other attributes are for nothing without initiative and hard work. It doesn't solve all problems, but it seldom creates problems.

A great day's work has its own rewards. There is nothing as satisfying as knowing you have done your best. In addition to putting food on the table, clothes on your back, and a roof over your head, a day's work well done makes us feel good about ourselves and improves our self-respect. Fatigue from a long day's work, plus that feeling that "today I did my very best," usually makes for a good night's sleep. It makes us healthier. It makes us feel better. Food tastes better.

Sex is better. Time off is better. Everything is better when you work hard. (Dad's answer to every problem.)

Hard work earns the respect and goodwill of your fellow man and the gratitude of your family. It can be a joy in itself and is often the most rewarding thing in a person's life. It often gives more than a living – it gives life itself – life with meaning and purpose and happiness.

However, there was much more to my dad than work and being a provider. The demands on him were huge, with the responsibility of a large family which consisted of eleven children, the same wife that he loved and adored for sixty-one years, and twenty- four grandchildren. Mom and Dad started this family at the beginning of the Great Depression, which was challenging, to say the least.

There was much more to Dad than his brief death announcement in the local paper's obituary which stated: "He owned and operated the local Southern States Coop Farm Supply Store with his son Jack from 1950-1968, a graduate of Clemson College of Engineering in Clemson, South Carolina, and a veteran of World War I. He served as President of the Breckinridge County Farm Bureau for many years, was a fifty-year member of the Masonic Lodge, and was a Past Master and Thirty-Second Degree Mason. He was an active member and deacon of the Hardinsburg Baptist Church."

There was much more to Dad than he would ever tell you. He was a man of few words, but every word was meaningful. His word was his bond, and you knew he said what he meant and meant what he said. I never remember him cursing or telling off-color stories or dirty jokes. He never used alcohol or drugs. He did smoke until he developed smoker's bronchitis in his early forties, then discontinued the habit. He was so concerned for me that he offered to give me a gold watch upon graduation from high school if I would not smoke. I did not smoke, and he delivered the watch as promised. With his encouragement I have never smoked one cigarette or had one drink of alcohol for my entire life, which I now recommend.

He was a man's man, loyal and faithful. He took great pride in his family, community, country, and had a deep faith in God, becoming a Christian through the influence of my mother.

He was a very strict disciplinarian and seldom needed more than a stern glance to correct outrageous behavior. His face was expressive and his eyes a window to his soul, and you could read him easily whether it was his approval, disapproval, pride, love, humor, anger, disgust, firmness, gentleness, irritation, impatience, determination, or respect. He did command respect and was held in highest regard by all – his wife, his children, his contemporaries, his community, and his church. He was indisputably the head of the family, a position ordained by my mother. She taught all her children to respect his position. To be sure, both he and all his children knew that it was Mom's wisdom, love, and influence that were responsible for the man he became and the success he achieved.

Dad took great pride in his wife of sixty-one years and loved her dearly. He gave her total credit for their survival and success.

Dad had a special relationship with his five daughters, who admired him and loved him dearly. He was the kind of father that every daughter should have.

My younger sister, Linda (the eleventh child), a retired school teacher and the only daughter still living, recently wrote these words:

"Daddy was a man of few words, but I always knew when he was pleased. My visualization of him is in his lounge chair with a smile of pleasure, contentment, and pride for my mother and their family together. Family was his priority.

"My dad gave me protection, security, and provided for his family with hard work and sacrifice every day of his life. Because of his example, I received a work ethic clothed with honesty and integrity. The instruction and guidance of my parents led me to know my Heavenly Father. Because of them, we have a double blessing of a loving earthly and Heavenly Father.

"There were special things I did for my special Dad. On hot summer days when he was plowing in the sweltering sun, I would take him a bucket of ice-cold water to quench his thirst. When he came home in the afternoon, I would mix up a pitcher of 'Linda's Lemonade,' which he loved to his dying day. Why? It had a cup of sugar in it. He also delighted when I brushed his shiny black hair. As an extra, I kept his Sunday shoes polished.

"I was trusted with Daddy giving me his checkbook when I went to college. I never wanted to take advantage and carefully guarded his bank account. The trust factor was already established. Daddy loved my mother, children, grandchildren, and God beyond measure. Dad, you were one of the THE GREATEST!"

Being raised by a strict mother who was both mother and father, he never learned to say "I love you," but we all knew that he did have great love for all of us. It took me years to learn to say "I love you." Eventually I realized how important it is in building relationships.

We all knew he would give his life for us and he, in fact, did give every ounce of energy and effort he could muster to raise his nine surviving children. Mom said that every summer he would drop from 165 lbs. to 125 lbs. from the long hours of farm labor done in double time from before daylight to after dark.

He had great pride in his physician/son and great faith in my medical care, as did all the members of my family. On the day he died, when I was with him in the local hospital and he was struggling with each breath from a worn-out heart (congestive heart failure), he placed his hand on my forearm and said (his last words to me), "Bob, you are a good egg," which, according to Google, is an old-fashioned way of showing affection to a good person and was Dad's highest expression of love and respect. My last words to him were "I love you, Dad. I will miss you. See you in Heaven."

I am reminded of Mom and Dad every day by the lives and personalities of their nine children, twenty-four grandchildren, and many, many great-grandchildren who resemble them in so many ways. Their lives were exemplary and their contribution to humanity huge and extraordinary. They gave direction to my life. A country doctor couldn't ask for more.

Paul B. and Elmina Chambliss
Dr. Chambliss' parents
Ages 78 and 79

Breckinridge County Elementary and High School
1928-1965
Painted by Becky Taul

CHAPTER 4

Education

My education began at birth because, as I've said, my mother was a teacher all the time. Before I was old enough to remember, Mom was teaching me songs, poems, and nursery rhymes. As far back as I can remember, I was taken to bed at night upstairs along with my younger sister, Linda, and read to from two books. The first was a children's book, usually with a life lesson or adventure story or a history story to "stretch our minds." The second was from the Bible or Bible story book, followed by reciting our prayers, a kiss on the forehead and a "Good night – sleep tight – we love you." As she disappeared down the stairs with the oil lamp in hand, I remember the shadows of the banisters marching across the ceiling in the upstairs hall; then all was dark, and I would think about the stories until I fell asleep.

It was not practical or possible for me to go to kindergarten, which was optional. My mother was insulted when her friend told her what a disadvantage this was. She made sure we knew more than any kindergarten student when we went into the first grade. It was no contest.

I was so excited about starting school. We lived almost a mile from school and every student that lived less than one mile from school had to walk, no matter what the weather was like. There were four of us in school my first year, so we all walked together except for my brother Paul, who would always run on ahead of us.

We all went to the same school, with grades 1-12 being housed in the same building, except for the seventh and eighth grades which had overflowed into a tar paper- covered temporary annex in the back. There was also a special unit for Vocational Agriculture.

My first-grade teacher was Miss Pauline Basham, a spinster, who taught first grade for over forty years. She had the reputation of being the best teacher in school. I loved her, and she would give me a hug when I walked in each morning. When I returned to Breckinridge County to practice medicine, she became my patient, as did every one of my grade-school teachers who were still there and most of my high-school teachers, even my dear friend Mrs. Eliza Payne, who knew I really didn't understand a single one of her algebra problems. They all placed their lives in my hands, which was a pleasant surprise and one of the most gratifying things in my practice. I even delivered a baby for one of my former teachers. I must have made the grade in more ways than on the report card (which was nearly always all A's). I loved school.

Miss Pauline gave each student who made all A's all year a new one-dollar bill. She also gave those with a perfect attendance record for the year a dollar. I had perfect attendance until the last day. I woke up completely covered with a measles rash. My mother sent word to Miss Pauline and she told her if she would have my father drive me to school in our old 1940 Chevrolet, she would count me present and come to the car and give me the new dollar bill. Two dollars in one year! I was rich! Little did I know how truly rich I was!

I didn't have any trouble keeping up with the privileged kinder-garten graduates, but I learned right away that "girls are smarter than boys," at least in the first grade. There were four or five in my class who surpassed my achievements--at first, anyway.

One of the girls, Wilma Basham, not only later became our high school valedictorian, but was first in her college graduating class in Home Economics at the University of Kentucky. She and I were the only ones in our class to go to college. It was fortunate for me that she was our pacesetter. I was very competitive (like my mother) and throughout the twelve years of school I achieved much more trying to keep up with her. Another smart girl from a rural school, Bobbi Haynes, joined us our freshman year and was our salutatorian, leaving me in third place.

I remember, as if it were yesterday, the first day of school. One of the boys came in a little late, squalling for his mother and holding on to her leg. Even after being pulled away, he cried all day for his mother. This scene was repeated for a month before he settled in. He also became my patient when I returned home, and my twelve years of growing up with him helped me immeasurably in learning how to treat his emotional problems. We were good friends and like so many classmates, he has predeceased me.

Mrs. Milburn was my second-grade teacher and the only teacher who had moved away by the time I returned to Hardinsburg. My most vivid memory of the second grade was breaking my arm on the playground. I was always adventuresome and somewhat of a daredevil and decided to walk across the top of the swing set like a tight rope walker. After two or three successful runs, I fell off and hurt my arm in the elbow. I decided to tough it out and not tell anyone, but after an hour or so Mrs. Milburn noticed tears rolling down my cheeks and notified my parents. They took me to our family physician, Dr. John E. Kincheloe's office, which was located in the back of the pharmacy on Main Street, in Hardinsburg. Dr. John A. Kincheloe, his son and 3rd generation physician, painfully reduced the fracture and applied a plaster cast. This was my first visit to a doctor's office. I still remember the distinctive medicinal odor, much like formaldehyde and alcohol.

My third-grade teacher was Clara Belle Dehaven, who must have been in her seventies at the time. I remember that on the first day she said, "Boys and girls, it doesn't make any difference how good your clothes are or what you wear in my class, but I do expect you to always wear clean clothes." I wore mostly bib overalls at the time, but I felt good because my mom always had our clothes clean and pressed. No problem! Miss Clara Belle was from the old school and believed in teaching "reading, writing and arithmetic." She believed everything else would fall in place.

My fourth-grade teacher was Naomi Fentress, a good teacher and strict disciplinarian who kept her paddle on the desk always and used it frequently. In time, she would become one of my most loyal patients and supporters.

My fifth-grade teacher was Janie Howard, age nineteen, teaching on an emergency certificate after two years of college. It was 1948 and I remember I tried very hard to learn more about the subjects and current events than she knew. I was told that she went to the principal and asked him to advance me to the sixth grade because she thought I knew more than she did. I probably was "getting on her nerves." That was my motive. Her request was not granted, and we spent the year competing. Years later, we were best friends, and as my patient she never questioned my treatment. Life has its little surprises.

My sixth-grade teacher was Mrs. Lucille Beauchamp, who was feared by all. She tolerated no nonsense. She was my neighbor, and I remember once when I was three or four years old, my parents had some kind of emergency and took my sister and me to her house until they returned the next day. I remember vividly at bedtime she put me in the bed between her and her husband, and I was horrified. I couldn't believe I was going to have a teacher I had slept with. I certainly didn't tell anyone!

Since I was her neighbor, she always expected more from me than from any of the other students. Not only academically, but I was always first in line for her paddlings. One day she was in my office to have three or four sebaceous cysts removed from her scalp. She was lying on the operating table and I was preparing to give her a local anesthetic. She said, "Bobby, do you remember all those paddlings I used to give you?"

I replied, "Yes, ma'am, I remember every one of them."

She replied teasingly, "You wouldn't hold it against me, would you?" We had a good laugh.

She was one of the many who made sure I was brought up "the right way." No foolishness! She was a hard taskmaster – learning was her objective in life. I was so glad to finish her class.

When I returned to school the next fall, I was disappointed to learn she had been assigned to the seventh grade. Her first words were, "I remember the 'School's out, school's out....' chant from last spring. We are going to work twice as hard this year."

Mrs. Beauchamp was 5 ft. 11 in. and weighed over 200 lbs. at least. We had a classmate who was a juvenile delinquent that they put in Mrs. Beauchamp's class--on purpose, I'm sure. I became a good fighter just defending myself from him on the playground. One day he was disturbing the class, and Mrs. Beauchamp told him to sit down. When he refused, Mrs. Beauchamp went back to his chair to force the issue. The student hit her in the abdomen with his fist as hard as he could. Mrs. Beauchamp grabbed him, lifted him up about two or three feet off the floor and jammed him into his seat. He turned white as a sheet and was deathly silent the rest of the afternoon. He eventually died a hardened criminal in the state penitentiary. Mrs. Beauchamp never needed any help with classroom discipline. We were impressed!

My eighth-grade teacher was Mrs. Brown, wife of E.D. Brown, Superintendent of Schools. She was very refined and quiet but a good teacher with high standards. I wasn't too academic by the time I got to her, because basketball now dominated my life and ambitions.

In high school I majored in extracurricular activities. The day was divided into six periods and required four subjects a year or sixteen credits to graduate. One period was designated as a study hall, which I took advantage of and got all my homework done so I wouldn't be bothered with it after school, and it wouldn't interfere with basketball. Basketball practice started the sixth period, forty-five minutes before school was out, and continued for another two or three hours after school.

When I was a senior, I still hadn't taken American history, which was a required credit to graduate. It was taught the sixth period. The coach wasn't about to have his leading scorer miss basketball practice and was successful in getting the principal to make an exception for me, and I graduated from high school with no exposure to American history. Basketball reigns supreme in Kentucky! I was at least forty years old before I developed an interest in history but have made up for it by being a prolific reader and very interested in history, especially World War II, because of my two older brothers' involvement.

My parents were very history-oriented, and I learned most of my history early on from them. They were proponents of the philosophy that you needed to know the past to keep from making the same mistakes in the future.

My dad allowed me to play basketball on one provision – that I keep up my farm chores. I got up before daylight to milk the dairy cows that provided milk for our large family. At night I was responsible for feeding all the livestock, so many times I fed in the dark. I kept up my end of the bargain, and he would fill in occasionally when the team or other school activity took me out of town. He grumbled a little bit, but I knew he was very proud of me.

Academics took a back seat in high school. I still made mostly A's but only because I paid attention in class, remembering almost everything, and did my homework at school. My grade-school academics were carrying me!

I had two interests: basketball and agriculture, which included FFA (Future Farmers of America). In both areas I had some spectacular teachers who influenced my life. The three top individuals were all men, which is a bit unusual.

My first coach in high school was T. L. Plain, who went on to be a member of the coaching staff at the University of Kentucky and eventually head basketball coach at the University of Utah. Charlie Yates was my agriculture teacher, one of Kentucky's best, who always made sure his students were competitive or number one in state activities.

R. F. Peters was principal and taught senior English literature. He was an accomplished scholar recognized as an authority in Shakespearian literature. He exposed us country boys to some higher learning and made us like it. He, like Mrs. Beauchamp, was a strict disciplinarian. We were always fear-struck when he would call us to his office. One day when I was a senior I heard the loudspeaker blurt out, "Bobby Chambliss come to the office, please." With fear and trembling, I went up the stairs to his office. He said to me, "Bobby, I have been watching you as you have progressed through high school. I think you can be anything you want to be, so set your sights high. That's all I wanted to say." Then he returned to his desk work. A seventeen-year-old boy never forgets something like that. Mr. Peters was the most learned and intellectual man I had known up to that time of my life. If he said it – it must be true. I treasured his statement and have always tried to emulate him by being an encourager.

I must have been a leader, because my class elected me president grades 6 through 12. I was captain of the basketball team and president of the FFA and eventually a state officer (our high school's first). My strength was in public speaking, and I won several speaking contests.

By the time I was a senior, I realized I would never play basketball for the University of Kentucky even though I had led our team in scoring three consecutive years as a sophomore, junior, and senior. I set a new school scoring record of 43 points in one game, averaged 19.1 points per game as a senior, and had made All District, and the Coaches Times-Argus, Messenger all 4th Regional Team. My total varsity scoring for the three years was 1426 points.

I had the opportunity to play for a state tournament team as a freshman. I was the smallest player in the state tournament. We won the district championship three of the four years I was in high school. My freshman year we won the regional tournament and went to the state tournament.

I was obviously too slow and too short. I could, however, hit over 50% of my shots from anywhere on the floor as the result of shooting a million times or more at a goal I nailed to the side of our chicken house and later in the barn loft. I was also eager and aggressive. I remember two events that show how eager and aggressive I was to advance in basketball. On the first occasion, I was in the eighth grade. I had had a good year and the last game of the season as a reward, the coach, T. L. Plain, let me dress out with the high school JV squad. There was about two minutes to go in the game and Coach Plain motioned for me to go in. I charged out onto the floor and the referee stopped me and said I couldn't come in because I had the same number on my jersey as one of my teammates.

As quick as a flash I took the jersey off and said, "I'll be a skin," as we often practiced as "shirts versus skins." It tickled the referee, so he stopped the game and let them find me a new jersey. I made four points and received a great ovation and much laughter.

The second occasion was at the beginning of my sophomore year in high school. We had graduated most of the varsity the year before and lost our star player due to a tragic near-fatal motor vehicle accident. It was unavoidable that we would have to start three sophomores.

After six weeks of practice, the coach hadn't named his starters. One day in practice there was a loose ball on the floor, and I dove between two players in front of me to get to the ball. The coach blew his whistle and stopped the practice and said, "Chambliss, you are my first starter" and gave us a lecture on "hustle."

I started the next 113 games over a period of three seasons, which may be some sort of record. I'm sure no one kept up with this, but it was important to me. One night at Hawesville I had a temperature of 103 and strep throat. I didn't tell the coach, but after 2-3 times up and down the court, I was shot. The coach said, "What's wrong with you, Chambliss?" I confessed, "I've got a sore throat and a temperature of 103." The coach sat me down, but I had kept my starting streak going!

Fifty years later, a former high school basketball player from a neighboring town came to my office as a patient and said to me, "Bobby, you were the most aggressive player I have ever played against." Enough said! This is the type of aggressive behavior I would need to get through medical school.

If I couldn't play for the University of Kentucky, I wouldn't play for any smaller college. I finally gave up my dream and turned my attention to my other dream— the secret I hadn't shared with anyone. I'll tell you that secret in the next chapter!

The last two years of high school, after I had received my driver's license, I purchased an old beat-up '46 Ford to provide my own transportation. The purchase was made from the Blancett Motor Co. in Hardinsburg. I remember well J. C. Blancett called my father to see if it was permissible. My father told him I had earned my own money and that I was a responsible boy and it met with his approval.

The purchase price was $300 and I kept it running and repaired at minimal expense for two years. It didn't have any attraction for girls in the community, but I had no time for dating anyway. I worked every spare minute to earn "college money," even carrying out groceries at Kroger's in Hardinsburg.

The day before I left for college, I drove to the Butler Garage and Salvage Yard on the other side of the family farm and asked Mr. Paul Butler what he would give me for the car. He looked it over and said, "Bobby, I'll give you $60 cash." Without a minute's hesitation I said, "Sold" and he took out his billfold and gave me $60 cash. I pocketed the money and walked across the farm to our house and started packing. No papers exchanged hands. The car ended up on the salvage yard.

I pocketed the money with a smile, knowing I had sent in my tuition for the first semester at the University of Kentucky the previous month. The tuition at that time was (you guessed it) $60.

My motto, as usual, was "Never look back." With hard work, my savings account, war bonds, and scholarships earned, I was sure I could make it (with a little luck). I was determined to make it on my own. My parents had sacrificed enough raising and educating nine children, and my "little sister," Linda, right behind me would need some assistance. She ended up becoming a teacher for thirty-two years, specializing in handicapped children. I know now my parents helped me more than I acknowledged at the time, but I was stubbornly independent, and they encouraged it and took pride in it, never complaining of the lifetime of hard work they had devoted to their large family.

So, I was off to a higher institution of learning, which I chose on the basis of their basketball team. Fortunately for me, they were also strong in academics. If I couldn't play basketball for the University of Kentucky, I certainly could go to school there and watch every game the team played. Adolph Rupp was still coach and won another national championship my second year at the University of Kentucky with the Fiddling Five. I lived in the quadrangle dormitories with many of the players and was thrilled with their achievements and my association with them.

Freshmen couldn't play on the varsity at that time, and they played a freshman schedule with the games starting at 5:00 p.m., before the varsity game. I was always watching front and center, and Kentucky always had a freshman team that was probably good enough to be ranked in the top 10 nationally in the varsity division. I was in heaven, and I have been an ardent fan all my life. I have attended ten or twelve "Final Fours," with the exception of the 1958 championship team when I was at the university. The finals were in Louisville, and I didn't have enough money to get from Lexington to Louisville; nor did I have enough money to buy a ticket. I made up for it later on by attending Final Fours at San Diego, San Antonio, St. Louis, Indianapolis, New Orleans, and Houston, just to name a few. Basketball has occupied a prominent and enjoyable part of my being – all my life!

CHAPTER 5

More About Education

On August 29, 1946, at the age of nine, I first thought I would become a physician. It was at "The Dr. John E. Kincheloe Day" in Breckinridge County in appreciation of his forty-seven years of service providing medical care for Breckinridge County, including the delivery of 5,496 babies (including me). There were 2,000 people in attendance at our local school campus, grades 1-12. Six hundred and sixty-five of us were proudly tagged, wearing a small card with the words "Kincheloe Baby," and our names written in the space provided. I wore mine proudly, because I admired our family physician. So did many others. Many babies in Breckinridge County were given the first or second name Kincheloe--some of them were still living when I returned home years later, "ready to take his place."

It was the biggest and most important celebration I had ever attended, with noted physicians and politicians from all over the state of Kentucky in attendance. The day was dedicated to the beginning of a fund to build a hospital in Breckinridge County. I paid attention to every word spoken praising Dr. John, as we all affectionately called him. I knew what he meant to me and listened to each testimonial and congratulatory speech that day. I learned that he was held in high regard and was appreciated by all our county residents. I was impressed.

Near the end of that day, I remember it going through my mind: *I think I will be a doctor.*

I never told anyone. It would be my secret ambition. Even at that age, I had observed children and their parents speak of their aspiration to become a physician, and despite being a nine-year-old, I knew they had no way of measuring up to it. But I kept it in my mind and close to my heart. It influenced my quest for academic achievement, and it influenced me to work hard for "college money," which I saved and guarded for that "maybe possible day." I did not realize that my success had a great deal to do with the intelligence of my mother and father, which had been passed down to their son.

I simply decided to apply myself, and if and when I proved I was up to the challenge, only then would I tell my family and friends, not a day sooner. And I stuck to it.

I bloomed in college. I took care of the academics and maintained a good grade point average, which I knew I would have to do to get into medical school. As I had in high school, I continued to be very interested in extracurricular activities. My freshman year I was active in the Future Farmers of America, having been elected State Secretary at the convention in Louisville that summer after I graduated from high school (our school's first state officer). This involved giving speeches all over the state of Kentucky at annual high school FFA banquets.

After my first year, I decided to join a social fraternity, choosing SAE, Sigma Alpha Epsilon, (one of eighteen), because they dominated campus inter-fraternity sports activities. This opened up a lot of opportunities. I became interested in student government and organized a new campus political party, which became very strong. After my junior year, I was the odds-on favorite to win the election for student government president as a senior. This was solidified when I was selected as the Outstanding Student at the University of Kentucky belonging to a fraternity. I was "crowned god" of Greek Week, which increased my chances of becoming student body president my senior year.

Two things happened that changed my plans and ambitions at the University of Kentucky. I got accepted to medical school after my third year of college, and the previous summer I had fallen in love with a wonderful Baptist girl from Hawesville, Kentucky who would soon graduate from Campbellsville Junior College. Suddenly nothing at UK mattered anymore. It was time to get on with my life.

Back then, Vanderbilt Medical School each year encouraged Dean White of the University of Kentucky College of Arts and Sciences to send them the top four third-year pre-medical students from the University of Kentucky to finish their BS or BA degree by combining it with the first year of medical school. This is called getting a degree in absentia. This ensured that Vanderbilt would get UK's top four premedical students, and it saved the students one year's cost of their education.

I had been the fortunate recipient of one of the four prestigious statewide Keeneland Agricultural Scholarships, which made it possible for me to attend college. There were few scholarships available in 1956. I entered the College of Agriculture Pre- Veterinarian program at the University of Kentucky. The pre-vet and pre-med curriculums were almost identical, except for a few agriculture courses. The pre-med curriculum had a few required humanities classes which I signed up for instead of the agriculture courses, because I still had becoming a physician in mind.

At the end of my second year in the College of Agriculture, I had yet to take an agriculture class and Stanley Walls, Dean of the

College of Agriculture called me to come to his office. I had known Dean Walls since I had served as State Secretary of the Kentucky Association of the Future Farmers of America my freshman year at UK.

Dean Walls told me that it was obvious to him my career was pointed toward medicine and not agriculture. He suggested I transfer to the College of Arts and Science and I admitted to him that I had been depending on the Keeneland Agriculture Scholarship to stay in school, along with carrying out groceries at Krogers. He also suggested that I write Keeneland and ask if they would continue my scholarship in The College of Arts and Science with a pre-med emphasis, and I did. I emphasized to the directors my rural background and my intent to return to rural Breckinridge County to practice medicine. The Keeneland Directors not only continued the scholarship through college, but continued it all the way through medical school. This was one of my early experiences with random acts of kindness. I will be eternally grateful!

I married that summer and moved to Nashville, where I would enter Vanderbilt Medical School. My wife, Janet, had been equally busy at Campbellsville College, where she was a cheerleader and active in the Baptist Student Union (BSU). She got a job at the Southern Baptist Sunday School Board in Nashville, which provides literature for the Southern Baptist Convention headquartered in Nashville, Tennessee.

Our interest in those happy carefree college days rapidly disappeared, and we were ready for more serious endeavors as we headed for Nashville and Vanderbilt Medical School – happy, madly in love, and unafraid. Our childhoods quickly became only happy memories and together as partners we were ready to get on with training for our life's work, family, and preparation for what we both felt was God's purpose for our lives.

So in August 1959, with a new wife, tuition paid, apartment rent paid, and $100 in my pocket, I entered the prestigious Vanderbilt School of Medicine with the same mindset as when I was a boy: "I'll see if I can make the grade." The class of fifty students was allegedly made up of forty-five Phi Beta Kappas. My work was cut out for me.

THIRTEENTH DISTRICT CHAMPIONSHIP TROPHY is accepted by Bearcat Captain Bobby Chambliss from Hancock County Superintendent Glover.

Bearcats Win District Tournament

by Graham E. Beard

Before the largest crowd of the tournament, the Breckinridge County Bearcats again proved their superiority by stomping the Irvington Tigers, 82-61. Irvington started off hot and took an early lead. Breckinridge County playing very consistently soon caught up with them and tied the score 17-17 at the end of the first stop. In the second quarter, the Tigers set up a stalling offense trying to pull the guards down the middle with the intention of collecting free throws. The Bearcats took care of this with a sinking defense and took advantage of every error. They pulled out with a seven point lead 38-31 at the half. Breckinridge County hit 47 percent of their field shots for these two quarters.

The second half started out in the same order with the Bearcats steadily pulling away. Chambliss came through with 8 straight points in the third quarter to give the Bearcats a safe margin for the rest of the game. At this stop, the Bearcats led 55-42.

In the final quarter with coach Parson substituting freely, the Bearcats continued to add to their margin. When the final buzzer was heard, Breckinridge County was on top by a margin of 82-61, which made them the undisputed champion of the thirteenth district.

The officials, Jack and Gene Gaither, called 21 fouls on Irvington, while Breckinridge County only got 15. Both teams lost one man on the foul route. At the foul line the Bearcats hit 26 out of 36 for 72 percent. The Tigers got 77 percent by hitting 23 out of 30. Breckinridge County got 28 field goals out of 53 attempts for 53 percent. The Tigers only got 19 which accounted for most of the 21 point margin between the two teams.

This is the fifth district championship for Breckinridge County in the last six years. The Bearcats, never chosen as the favorites of the district year after year by the local sports writers, always seem to emerge as the victor. This year Breckinridge County won as the result of defeating the three supposedly toughest teams of the district. The scores were Breckinridge County 76 - Hawesville 76, Breckinridge County 61 - Flaherty 59; and Breckinridge County 82 - Irvington 61.

On the all-tournament team the winners, Breckinridge County, only placed one man, Ronnie Pile, their flashy Sophomore center.

Bobby Chambliss, senior member of the Bearcats squad was not only high scorer of the tournament, but was also the leading rebounder. He was followed by Ronnie Pile, who was second and Charlie Robinson, third in tournament scoring.

Scoring for the final game was as follows:

Bearcats (82) Chambliss 22, Pile 20, Beard 21, Robinson 14, Dowell 3, Brite 2, Bruington D. 0, Bruington R., 0.

Tigers (61) Johnson R., 21, Carman 10, Brumfield 9, Johnson, A., 8, Basham 7, Pollock 5, Smith, R. 1.

Breckinridge County plays Centertown at 8:30 on Thursday night in the regional tournament which is to be at Morgantown.

In the last home tilt of the season, Bobby Chambliss, senior captain of the squad, scored 43 points to lead the Bearcats to an impressive 99-82 victory over Centertown. This win avenged an earlier loss to the Demons. Chambliss set a new record in his last home game.

Breckinridge County had teamwork from the first till the last in one of the best games they have played so far. They never let up. At the first stop, they led 24-16. Hitting phenomenally and with great rebounding the Bearcats added to their margin and led 54-36 at the half. They hit 59 percent of their shots for the half.

In the last half, Breckinridge County cooled off some. Centertown also began to hit somewhat better. At the third stop the score was 77-59. The Bearcats set 100 as their goal in the last quarter. With seconds to go an the score at 99 they had the ball, but shot wide of the goal. This was the Bearcats' eighteenth win against six losses. By winning this game, Breckinridge County kept its home record clean.

At the foul line, the Bearcats hit 69 percent of 42 attempts. Centertown got 53 percent of 19 attempts. The Demons lost three man on fouls while Breckinridge County lost none. For the game, the Bearcats hit 51 percent of their field shots.

Officials: Macon and Long.

Breckinridge County won the preliminary game 43-30.

Individual scoring: Bearcats (99): Chambliss 43, Beard 21, Pile 17, Robinson 10, Dowell 8, Stiff 0, Brite 0, Bruington 0.

Demons (82) Russ 24, Tichenor, J., 20, Maddox 19, Brock 8, Tichenor, B., 4, Bennett 4, Snodgrass 3, Brown 0.

Bob Chambliss
Junior
University of Kentucky 1958

Janet Bruner Chambliss' photo that Dr. Chambliss kept on his desk from his Junior year at UK through medical school.

The Kentucky KERNEL

UNIVERSITY OF KENTUCKY

Vol. L   LEXINGTON, KY., THURSDAY, DEC. 4, 1958   No. 40

Darnell, Chambliss Reign Over Greeks

Susan Darnell was named outstanding sorority woman durin Greek Week festivities last week. She is pictured at the dan held in the Phoenix Hotel Saturday night.

Susan Darnell and Bob Chambliss were chosen Greek god and goddess last night at the convocation initiating Greek Week on the UK campus.

Susan is a senior English major and a member of Delta Delta Delta sorority. Her activities include Mortar Board, treasurer of Panhellenic Council, Chi Delta Phi, Tau Sigma, English Club and Philosophy Club.

Susan transferred to UK following her freshman year at Mount Holyoke College, So. Hadley, Mass. Her overall standing is 3.77.

Chambliss is a second semester junior in pre-med. He is a member of Sigma Alpha Epsilon fraternity. Chambliss has an overall standing of 3.25. He is a member of Keys, Lances, ODK, Pryor Pre-Med Society, Phalanx, SU Board and IFC.

Chambliss was awarded a $2,000 Keeneland scholarship. He was chairman of the fall Leadership Training Program for freshmen.

Also at the convocation last night at Memorial Hall, Ollie James, chief editorial writer and columnist for the Cincinnati Enquirer, was guest speaker.

James, a graduate of UK and an alumnus of Sigma Nu fraternity,

Continued On Page 8

Greek Week festivities closed with the Four Freshmen concert Friday night and the God and Goddess Ball Saturday night.

The Freshmen, performing before an audience of 2,500 at Memorial Coliseum, mixed a variety of moods, rhythm, and styles to keep the undivided attention of their audience. They selected some of their favorite recordings such as "Malaya," "Angel Eyes," "Sweet Lorraine," "There'll Never Be Another You," and "Granada."

Clyde Trask, his orchestra, and singer Betty Ann Blake were also

included in the program. Among Miss Blake's selections were such standards as "Moonlight In Vermont," "I Get a Kick Out of You" and "Foggy Day."

The Freshmen are composed of two brothers, Don and Ross Barbour from Columbus, Ind., a cousin, Bob Flanigan, Greencastle, Ind., and Ken Albers, Wenonah, N. J.

A capacity crowd filled the Phoe-

nix Hotel's Convention Hall and the Gold Room for the God and Goddess Ball Saturday night. The rooms were decorated with Greek columns and ivy.

Buddy Morrow played for the ball. Bob Chambliss, outstanding fraternity man, and Susan Darnell, outstanding sorority woman, were crowned by IFC President Bill Kincaid.

Greeks

Continued From Page 1

has spoken to a number of fraternity groups previously.

The scheduled Greek Week activities will resume tomorrow night with a concert at the Coliseum, featuring the Four Freshmen and the Clyde Trask orchestra.

Tickets to the concert, which is open to the public, are $1.50 per person. Sections will be reserved for each Greek organization.

Greek Week festivities will end Saturday night with the god and goddess dance at the Phoenix Hotel. Buddy Morrow and orchestra will play for the dance, which is for greeks and their dates only. Dancing will be in the ballroom and tables will be set up in the Gold Room.

The students were picked by a faculty committee composed of Dr. Leslie L. Martin, dean of men; Dr. Doris M. Seward, dean of women; John Profitt, assistant to the dean of men; Mrs. Sharon Hall, assistant to the dean of women; Mrs. Sarah B. Holmes, former dean of women; Dr. A. D. Kirwan, professor of history and former dean of men, and Dr. James Gladden, professor of sociology.

Their choices were based on qualities of scholarship, leadership and contribution to the greek system.

Each greek group nominated three outstanding members and a council of Panhellenic and Interfraternity council members limited the finalists to ten outstanding sorority women and 13 fraternity men. Final choice was left to the faculty group.

Greek of the Year: Bob Chambliss of Kentucky Epsilon holding trophy he won at the University of Kentucky, Lexington.

CHAPTER 6

Medical School

Medical school was a job! There were no extracurricular activities other than going to church on Sunday morning. I took the job seriously, which was to learn as much medicine as I could every day so that someday someone could trust me to do the job proficiently. I gave it my best shot every day, and fortunately had a memory that could assimilate massive amounts of information, and enough common sense to know what was relevant, practical, and useful.

Knowing my competition, I studied very hard, sometimes until 2:00 a.m. It paid off; at the end of my first semester in gross anatomy I was told I was leading the class (the only time I ever led a class.)

The second semester we studied biochemistry that involved a research project where we fed hundreds of white rats certain diets and then killed them (necropsy) and took out their livers and ran tests to determine how different diets affected their livers and leads to certain diseases and causes of death. I hated it! I had already had enough experience killing rats in the corn crib and hen house on the farm, and I wasn't interested in research.

I discovered that semester that Vanderbilt was a research-oriented school whose objective was to turn out specialists, researchers, and academic-oriented physicians. They were not interested in their graduates entering family practice or becoming country doctors (my ambition).

Why didn't Vanderbilt know this was my ambition? I had been interviewed by a member of the Medical Student Selection Committee, a physician whose name I have forgotten. Early on in the interview, the interviewing professor read in my application that I had been accepted to the Omicron Delta Kappa Senior Honorary Society at the University of Kentucky as a junior. I related to him that Jesse Stuart, famous Kentucky author, was inducted as an honorary member on the same night, and I sat next to him and my parents at the front banquet table at the Campbell House in Lexington; we became good friends. The interviewing professor seemed impressed. He had been president of ODK at Vanderbilt when he was a student.

He also asked me about being named the Outstanding Student belonging to a Fraternity at the University of Kentucky. I was a member of SAE, Sigma Alpha Epsilon Social Fraternity. I didn't tell him that I joined SAE because they were the "jock" fraternity at UK, and I wanted to play intramural basketball for them. I can't remember anything else we talked about. I was in! I left with the assurance of his recommendation for admission. The notice of acceptance came soon, and I accepted it.

After 4 ½ months of killing rats and overhearing the 4th-year medical students talking about not having been taught any practical medicine like how to treat simple strep throat, I began to realize I had chosen the wrong school. I had also been accepted by the University of Louisville. The new University of Kentucky Medical School was not due to open until the fall of 1960. I didn't want to wait, and I didn't want to be in the first class at the University of Kentucky Medical School. I admit, I was also very impressed by the prestige of having been accepted by Vanderbilt.

As is my nature, I went to the Dean of Medicine at Vanderbilt Medical School and told him my ambitions and shared my feeling that I was at the wrong school. Much to my relief, he understood. He said, "Bob, the University of Tennessee in Memphis has a reputation for turning out the best rural physicians in the nation and takes pride in supplying the state of Tennessee with above-average general practitioners." He went on to say, "I'm a good friend of the Dean of Medicine at UT Medical School and if you would like, I will call him and discuss a transfer. Since you are in the upper third of your class here at Vanderbilt, I think he would accept you in the 4th quarter at UT." I agreed; and he called the dean in my presence, and I was accepted immediately. Imagine that! The dean at Vanderbilt wished me a happy successful career. I thought at the time, *Every time I get off track, God sends somebody to get me back on track.*

We went directly to Memphis and entered the 4th quarter (summer quarter) in July and never looked back. I went to school year-round, and because of gaining a year leaving UK at the end of three years and going straight through medical school without a summer break, I finished college and medical school in six years and three months, graduating in an off month of March, 1963. For most students it takes eight years to get through college and medical school.

The University of Tennessee School of Medicine was on the quarter system – four three-month quarters annually. They accepted fifty students per quarter, or two hundred new students every year. Little did I know, however, that they didn't hesitate a second to have you repeat a quarter if you did not do well or have you leave school if you did poorly.

Indeed, I discovered that I had left a medical school with the philosophy "If we accept you – we know you are ok and we intend to graduate you" for a school that would show you the door in a heartbeat if you did not produce. That made it very competitive, and I had to study harder than ever in a competitive situation.

But Janet and I had each other, and that was all that mattered. We had no doubts that we could make it. She made a whopping $300 per month, and I had been granted a Kentucky Rural Scholarship loan awarded to those who promised to practice in rural Kentucky when they finished medical school, which was my original plan anyway.

We lived in a mobile home in Nashville and later in Memphis until I finished my MD degree. By living extremely frugally, we made it. At the end of each quarter, we would treat ourselves to $1.99 steak dinner at Walgreens. Love and future expectations went a long way, and we were ever so happy.

After two years, we began to think of starting a family. We decided to have our first child in my last year of medical school. We stopped the birth control pills one month, and the next month she was pregnant. I had been studying birth control in Ob/Gyn classes and thought I was ready to start giving lectures. The second pregnancy came during my internship at Louisville General Hospital and definitely was not planned. So much for the birth control lectures. Jim was born 13 ½ months after Bryan, right in the middle of my internship, which was not an opportune time. Those two were like twins and kept my wife occupied while I was working thirty-six hours on and twelve hours off at Louisville General Hospital for a grand salary of $100 a month. There was a time when interns and residents were not paid anything in return for the privilege of getting their training at a teaching hospital. Your training was pay enough! Today the salaries are very generous, and the hours worked are more humane. The last pregnancy was planned four years later while we were in Cumberland County and again right on schedule.

I chose to intern at the Louisville General Hospital because of their reputation for teaching you more practical hands-on medicine than any other hospital in mid-America. I also chose them because all my attending (teaching) physicians would be physicians I would be referring to when I started practice out in the state, with Hardinsburg being only sixty miles from Louisville. I wanted to know them, and I wanted them to know me. This was one of the best decisions I ever made! Little did I know at the time that the Louisville General Hospital paid only $100 a month.

General Hospital let me start my internship in April 1963 and continue until March 30, 1964, an off time to be sure, but they were low on interns because the 4th-year class prior to my arrival there had a dispute with the University of Louisville Medical School and the Louisville General Hospital, and they all decided they would intern somewhere else. However, it worked well for me since I would get out another three months early. Also, there was more work for me to do, increasing my experiences, since we had a limited number of interns. When I finished, I was told I would be Kentucky's youngest practicing physician.

During our year of internship, we had continued to live in our 46-foot, single-wide mobile home we had first lived in at Nashville. We moved it to Memphis and then to a trailer park in Jeffersonville, Indiana, just across the bridge from Louisville, Kentucky. It was only a short distance across the bridge to downtown Louisville where General Hospital was located on Chestnut Street. It was an old building at that time and has since been torn down.

Bryan, our oldest son, was born at the John Gaston Teaching Hospital in Memphis, TN on 10/10/1962 in a special suite and labor rooms set aside for hospital doctors in training, interns, and medical students. It was provided to us at no cost, so we took advantage of it. Jim was born at Jewish Hospital in Louisville, Kentucky on 11/27/1963 during my internship, very conveniently on the day I was to present Grand Rounds to the entire hospital staff – a traumatic event every intern dreaded, because we had to present our treatment of an interesting patient we had taken care of and defend our treatment. There would be over 100 staff members, residents, interns, and medical students in attendance. This was a traumatic day for an intern or resident. Because Janet was in labor, they excused me to be with her and my resident took over. Jim started life doing me a great favor!

When I finished at age twenty-six, I didn't look a day older than eighteen. I wasn't about to return to my hometown, which was my lifelong ambition, until I got some experience somewhere else.

In January 1964, I went to the Kentucky Medical Association Building in Louisville and met with Bobby Grogan, acting Executive Director of the Kentucky Medical Association. Bobby had an agriculture background and had supervised our 1956-57 state Future Farmers of America Officer's team. I asked Bobby to tell me which county in Kentucky needed a physician more than any other county, and I would go there. I had been the recipient of a Kentucky Rural Medical Scholarship Loan and was obligated to go somewhere in rural Kentucky. As an incentive, for every year I practiced medicine in a "critical needs county" in Eastern Kentucky (should I choose to go there) I would be forgiven a year of my Rural Scholarship loan. In addition, I would also get more experience there than any other place in the state.

Bobby said two young doctors, Keith Kirby and Ted Beck, had just left a big practice in Cumberland County to specialize in anesthesia and radiology. Cumberland County is located in south central Kentucky in the foothills of the Appalachian Mountain chain. The office was unoccupied, the staff unemployed, waiting for the next doctor--and I would not have to build a practice. How true that turned out to be!

Dr. Chambliss takes his family to Burkesville, KY.
Janet, Bryan and Jim

Young doctor, age 26, and one of his first patients.

CHAPTER 7

Beginning of Practice

My intention was to stay in Cumberland County for two years and then move back to my hometown of Hardinsburg. So, with a young wife and two baby boys, I made my entrance into Burkesville on April 3, 1964. We were welcomed to Cumberland County and Burkesville by everyone. They thanked us profusely before we ever got started. Cumberland County was obviously a Critical Health Care County as designated by the Kentucky Medical Association and the State Legislature, who had established the rural loans for those who would go to these critical need counties, most of them in the Appalachian Region of Eastern Kentucky. Later, I would serve on this state committee.

We had gladly left our mobile home in Jeffersonville, Indiana, with a "For Sale" sign in front of it. It sold quickly, and we used the money to buy some very old medical equipment from a retiring physician in Scottsville, Kentucky. We gathered all our meager possessions, and some new Delker furniture my wife's Uncle Tom Glover, Mayor of Henderson, Kentucky, helped us buy at the local furniture factory, and loaded it all into a U-Haul truck. I drove the truck, and my wife followed in our very tiny Falcon Ford with the boys.

We moved into our new home and office. The office was located downtown across from the courthouse. The other two young doctors who had occupied it told us it had been converted from a previous pool room into a doctor's office. Legend has it that after becoming a doctor's office, there wasn't nearly as much blood shed on the premises as when it was a pool room. Janet moved into the house with the help of many volunteers, and I went directly to the office and went to work. The first day, in between straightening up and trying to find and organize everything, I saw some patients. My office staff was a veteran group. They knew everyone in town. They knew their medical history and their disposition. They were a great help in getting started, and I took their advice and cues.

For instance, the nurse whispered in my ear, "This grandmother told the receptionist she thinks her grandson has 'worms.'" So in addition to taking care of the child's problem, I added, "He looks like he is wormy; I gave her a prescription for worms. The grandmother left thinking I was pretty smart. I later learned that most of the kids in Cumberland County did, indeed, have worms and needed a "good worming" from time to time.

I saw 19 patients the first day, and before long that was up to 75-100 patients a day (24-hour day). I saved the physician day book from that first day for you to see. (See Appendix A). In fact, I have the day sheets covering a period of 53 going on 54 years. During this period of time I have seen over 700,000 patients!

Can you imagine $3 office visits, $5 house calls, and $10 for most x-rays? I charged $75 for a delivery at the nearest hospital, War Memorial in Albany, Kentucky, Clinton County. I didn't have a local hospital for the first two years there until the Cumberland County Hospital was completed. As I said earlier, I didn't look a day over eighteen, and despite the fact that I was six feet tall and weighed 170 lbs, I was immediately called "The little new doctor."

The reason soon became obvious. My competition in Burkesville was a seventy- plus-year-old physician who never welcomed any young doctor to Cumberland County. He was one of those physicians in Eastern Kentucky who got so much publicity in the '70s for seeing 100-150 patients a day and liked being the only doc in town. He had a large office downtown and had also built an annex onto his home where he could continue to see patients in the evening and all night long.

There was another elderly, ninety-five-year-old retired physician whose younger wife was an RN. She had always worked together with him, and they continued to see a few patients at their home.

Clinton County, the most accessible adjacent county, had two elderly docs that I estimated to be in their eighties, so I did, indeed, start out as "the little new doc."

It was only a few months after President Kennedy's assassination, our youngest- looking president ever, that I showed up in Cumberland County as the youngest-looking doctor ever!

I was young, but very, very confident. I had just completed my internship at Louisville General Hospital where I had been allowed to do anything I thought I was big enough to do--under supervision, of course. They had a motto there: "See one, do one, teach one."

I had been as aggressive and eager as an intern as I had been playing basketball. I tried to learn everything I could. For instance, I would watch an orthopedic resident reduce a fracture and he would say, "You do the next one," and I did! One Saturday evening we had a shootout in West Louisville, and they brought in ten men with multiple gunshot wounds to the chest and abdomen. They had only had eight operating rooms and fortunately, were able to round up eight surgical residents and staff surgeons. Two victims, the least hurt, were left in the hall on stretchers to wait their turn. I was assigned to one of the surgeons. He turned to me and said, "Bob, you give the anesthesia."

I replied, "I have never given anesthesia."

He replied, "It makes no difference; I'll talk you through it," and we got along well. That was my first anesthesia, and after that long night I never had any fear of doing it again and again. An interesting footnote – all ten of those patients recovered and lived to return to West Louisville only to do it again some future Saturday night.

We were given responsibility and given the green light as fast as we mastered the various skills. In fact, we were given more respect and trust from the patients than we deserved. One night when I was on psychiatry, I admitted a beautiful redheaded woman who was severely depressed. On rounds the next morning, our teaching professor was making rounds with us, and he interviewed and examined the patient and recommended that she should have EST (electric shock treatments). He asked her if she would accept the treatment and sign the permit. She said, "I don't know-I'll have to ask my doctor," and turned to me, a lowly intern. I told her I definitely thought it was the treatment of choice, and only then did she accept the treatment recommended by the head of the Department of Psychiatry.

My rotation through obstetrics was in November and December. At Christmas, all the students and many of the interns and residents went home for the holidays. The residents and interns remaining had already delivered all the babies they cared to deliver. I was young and aggressive, and I volunteered to deliver every woman who came in during the Christmas season. I had already been on obstetrics for one month, and everyone was impressed with the good training I had received at the University of Tennessee.

The interns and residents were more interested in sleeping than delivering more babies, so they said, "Go for it!" Louisville General Hospital back then delivered ten or fifteen indigent patients every twenty-four hours. I was eager to get all the experience I could get, knowing this would be a big part of my practice. For a week I stayed up day and night with just a "few winks" between babies.

The last night of the Christmas week vacation, after over 100 deliveries, I was gowned, masked, and gloved, sitting on a stool with the patient draped and in position for delivery. I was waiting for the baby's head to come down a little more for an easier application of forceps. As I was patiently and quietly waiting, I nodded off and fell over into the draped patient. The next thing that I was aware of was two nurses tilting me back up into a sitting position. Embarrassed and awake, I proceeded to deliver the patient uneventfully. I don't think the patient ever knew that I had gone to sleep on the job. The nurses declared it wasn't the first time they had awakened a doctor during a delivery. They knew I was embarrassed, and they complimented my endurance for the week and said I was the most skilled intern they had ever worked with. The nurses told me to go to bed, and they would call the resident on call for the next delivery. I had kept my end of the bargain. Imagine that! Over 100 babies delivered in one Christmas season.

I completed my internship in March of 1964. Four months later when I was in Burkesville getting my real training and having the time of my life, I was notified that the Annual Awards Banquet was coming up for the 1963/64 class and that I had been awarded the George P. Caldwell Award presented annually to the Louisville General Hospital intern showing the greatest proficiency of the year. I can assure you that I didn't win the award because I was the smartest. I won it because I worked the hardest and was the most aggressive and eager to learn as much as I could before going into a rural practice.

In Burkesville, I was already doing what I had always dreamed of doing. I had finished my internship three months before the rest of the class, because I graduated in the spring quarter class at the University of Tennessee Medical School and started my internship early. I was already busy, and I decided not to attend the annual banquet. I wrote a letter expressing my gratitude for being selected for the award and thanked them for the opportunity to intern at Louisville General Hospital. I also thanked them for the excellent practical training I had received there and told them I was already putting it to good use and was too busy to attend. They mailed me the certificate and news release, and it still hangs on my office wall with my other diplomas and awards.

In 1964 there was no such thing as a Family Practice Residency or Board Certified Family Practice Specialty. You went into practice immediately after your internship. Now you are required to take a three-year Family Practice Residency, and if you pass a difficult board exam, you become a Board Certified Family Practice Diplomat or have specialty status. For those of us who finished our training before the Family Practice Specialty was initiated, we were allowed to take the same board exam. Those who passed received the board certificate. I passed. This is called "grandfathering in." I still looked eighteen (young grandfather!).

Education for a physician does not end with an internship or residency. We are required by law to participate in continuing medical education (CME) to keep our license. The American Academy of Family Practice requires a designated number of CME hours annually, and the American Medical Association also has their recommendation. As usual, I have opted to take more hours than required and for all my career have attended CME seminars with more than fifty hours of classroom attendance each year. Add to this the many lectures which are presented by the local hospital, drug companies, and various medical groups, internet presentations, and others. The process of learning and keeping up is ongoing for a lifetime. It never stops.

Most physicians receive a number of medical journals which add to their knowledge and, of course, the answer to any medical problem is as close as your computer or apps on your smartphone, which are used on a daily basis. I would be remiss if I didn't mention that I have taught Sunday school for over forty years and the most- worn books in my library are my Bible and Bible commentaries.

Education begins at birth and ends at death. I am confident that physicians are the most dedicated group in our society to continue their lifetime of learning. I think the public is aware of this and rewards those physicians who are the most current with the rapidly expanding knowledge in the field of medicine. My real education was just beginning.

I will never forget Cumberland County and the education I got there. I stayed five years and three months and was barely able to get my wife to consent to moving back home. The good people of Cumberland County treated her like a queen, and she loved them. I loved them, too. They had a big "Going Home" party for us at the Cumberland Lake Lodge, and most of them wept as we said our goodbyes. My wife and I also wept that night as we returned to our first home in Burkesville, Kentucky.

CHAPTER 8

The Little New Doctor Who Laughed at Himself

STORIES ALONG THE WAY

The second day I was in Burkesville, I was called and asked to come out on Pea Ridge to see Granny Smith (not her name). I was only twenty-six years old, and at the time I didn't look a day over eighteen. I was told how to find Granny Smith's road eleven miles south of town. I was to meet a man at the mouth of the road who would show me how to find the cabin up in the hills. I found the man, and he looked into the car and said, "Be ye the doc?"

I placed my hand on the big new medical bag at my side (to help him with his doubt) and said, "Yes, I'm the doctor."

He got into the car and said, "I'll show you the way." He never said another word. We traveled 2-3 miles up a winding dirt road into the hills, finally coming to a clearing and, to my surprise, there were 10-15 old pick-up trucks and cars around a little two room cabin. I was to learn later that calling the doctor was a special occasion "in these parts," and everyone had come to see me "doctor Granny."

With medical bag in hand and looking as professional as I knew how to look, I said "Howdy" to each and every neighbor (about twenty of them) and approached Granny's bed and forthwith kicked over the pot (potty) under the edge of the bed. Everyone froze momentarily to see what I would do. So, knowing nothing better to do, I laughed, and they laughed, and then we all laughed heartily together. Those mountain people, who are by nature very reserved with strangers, decided right then and there that they liked the "little new doctor," as they would call me, who could laugh at himself. To this day before I approach a patient, I always check the side of the bed.

Taking care of sick people with all the stress, the sadness, the tragedies, the critically ill, the terminally ill, and the dying is serious business. It takes the best that is in us to do it. If we couldn't laugh at ourselves and with others – we couldn't stand up under the pressure. If we couldn't laugh – we couldn't survive!

So I am a big proponent of laughter therapy. The Bible says in Proverbs 17:22 "A merry heart doeth good like a medicine." *Readers Digest* for years has reminded us monthly that "Laughter Is the Best Medicine." Laughter not only keeps us healthy--it keeps us humble in the practice of medicine. Voltaire said, "The art of medicine consists of amusing the patient while nature cures the disease." Now that's humbling!

Self-deprecating humor is by far the most effective. Someone has said, "The noble secret of laughing at one's self is the greatest humor of all." Laughing at yourself can get you through some of the most awkward situations (for instance, the potty).

Early on in my practice I wanted to have all the experiences of a country doctor. I decided I would do a home delivery, so I started looking for a patient that would be an easy one. A lady that had had twelve children came in pregnant once again and asked for a home delivery. I had found my first home delivery – an easy one, I thought!

Luckily for me, she sent word that she was in labor on a Wednesday morning, my day off. I went to her home out on Pea Ridge and examined her and decided to wait at her home until she delivered. Her husband was a former moonshiner--for which Cumberland County is famous, dating back to Prohibition Days.

His wife was a very plump and pleasant lady. She had a very hard labor all day long, and I sat on the front porch and whittled and learned all about moonshining in Cumberland County. About dark she began to crown (head presenting) and struggled with that for about another hour. Before it was over, I was up in the bed with this lady, on my knees, pulling with all my strength. We were on a feather bed and she and I flattened out the middle of it and the sides of that feather bed folded up on both sides about covering us up. I finally backed out the other end spitting feathers with the baby and praising God that it was healthy. The baby had the biggest head I had ever seen on a newborn. Only then did I notice that the father had an unusually large head and six or eight little boys running around outside the cabin had big heads. I said to the lady, "Have you had hard labors before?" and she said, "Yes, sir, every one of them has been like this one." This young doctor learned some lessons that day that they had tried to teach me at medical school. Take a good history!

I also learned a good lesson in economics. The retired moonshiner said, "Doc, send me a bill. Send me a big one. Make it look good because I can't pay you anyway." I also learned another lesson later. The old doctors who delivered babies at home had portable leg stirrups, which would have made it a lot easier and a lot less comical.

One of my favorite stories from Cumberland County includes Martha and Joe. Martha weighed 585 lbs. Joe was 5'2." They lived about a mile outside of town and walked to town every day, Joe trailing Martha by about twenty feet. They had to go past the stockyards, and Martha would sometimes stop and weigh herself on the cattle scales. One day I was called to the emergency room to see Martha who had severe abdominal pain. I hurried over to the hospital where Martha was on the examining table moaning and groaning. I examined her abdomen which was a huge mound of fat. I couldn't tell anything for the fat. I then instructed the young ER nurse to put her up for a pelvic exam. It took a whole sheet to cover her legs and looked like a tent. It got up under the "tent" and started my exam. I quickly said, "Hmmm! I think I see what's wrong" and pulled out a squalling baby from under the sheet and laid it up on her huge belly. The little nurses were in shock. They thought I was playing some kind of trick on them.

Like everything in Burkesville, word got around fast, and when I showed up the next morning at the local restaurant where we all had breakfast, the guys were already laughing about it. They said, "Doc, we understand Martha having a baby. What we can't understand is how did Joe get her pregnant!"

I said, "Well, beats me!"

I was invited back to Cumberland County to speak at the 25th anniversary of the Cumberland County Hospital. I told the story about Martha and Joe. It just happened that Joe was still living and in the local nursing home attached to the hospital and the nurses on the night shift went back immediately and told Joe what I had said. Joe told them, "Tell Doc you have to have very special equipment." I had made his day! He couldn't care less about this HIPAA thing.

This is my all-time favorite fat story. It has been great fun down through the years listening to the things women say when they are in labor and under the influence of pain and pain medications and light anesthesia, especially the nitrous oxide we used back then. These disparaging remarks are usually directed toward their husbands! Once, a 300 lb.- plus lady was on the delivery table. She actually hung off both sides of the table. She said to me in a squeaky anesthesia-altered voice, "Dr. Chambliss, do you think I am too fat?"

Being honest, I said, "Well, yes, I think you are too fat."

To which she said, "Well, you don't look so hot yourself!" The nurses cracked up.

I will never forget a man I saw in the emergency room one night. He lived out in the country in a house that had no electric lights or indoor bathroom. It was a very dark night, and he felt nature's urge to go to the outdoor toilet one hundred feet behind the house. To light his path, he rolled up an old newspaper tightly, soaked the end in lamp oil, and set fire to that end, making a torch.

This particular outhouse was a two-seater. I have never understood why some outhouses had two seats – because I can't think of anyone I would want to sit beside when I go to the bathroom. My wife explains, "Anyone living in a house with four males would know the answer to that one." Nevertheless, on being seated, he laid the torch down by his side on the seat. As it burned down, it fell into the other hole, and there was an instant terrible explosion and fire that blew him off the seat and out the door and burned the outhouse to the ground.

He told me later he learned that they had been painting the barns that week and the painters had washed out their paint buckets and brushes with gasoline and emptied them into the privy. I could barely keep a straight face. If you have ever seen one of those red-tailed monkeys at the zoo, it would perfectly describe this man's posterior.

For months, any mention of this poor man would cause uncontrollable laughter around our hospital. It is the only time in my practice I can remember seeing blisters on hemorrhoids.

And then there's the story about the first and only lady I ever set on fire. It was over in Burkesville, the first year I was in practice. A lady came in with a mole on the back of her neck. The patients over there would often wear their very best clothes to the doctor's office. She came in wearing a sweater with long hair, about two inches long. Standing behind her, I started removing the mole with a hyfrecator, which is an electric arc. Suddenly the top of her sweater burst into brief flames, and I quickly patted it out with my hands. Fortunately, neither she nor I was burned badly, and she never knew that there was a flame involved. I had to tell her there was a little heat generated from the treatment and that I may have done a little damage to her sweater. I told her I would replace it if it was badly damaged. I did not try to explain the sudden patting of her shoulders with my hands. I don't know what she thought about that! I've always wondered what she thought of her sweater when she got home and found out that her long-haired sweater was now a short-haired sweater, especially on the shoulders. They have since taken flammable sweaters off the market.

Another time, they called me down to the local jail where one of my psychotic patients was lying on the cell floor, totally nude. They couldn't persuade her to get up and put her clothes on, so they called me, her family doctor. I went down to the jail and as authoritatively as I could I said, "Mary Sue [not her name] get up and put your clothes on."

She immediately got up and dressed. I heard the deputies laughing behind me and saying, "You know, Dr. Chambliss is really good at getting women to put their clothes on!" Now that's a reverse left-handed compliment!

My sister Mabel was an RN in Bowling Green and spent her life cheering people up and entertaining them with her Erma Bombeck-type personality. She had unbelievable tragedies in her life, including the death of two children in a car wreck and nearly losing her own life. Despite that, she maintained the sweetest spirit and a wonderful attitude. Like Dr. Buchele and Fonda Roach in my office, she had an unmistakable cackle and could laugh in the face of the devil himself. Other nurses loved to work with her.

Once she had an elderly post-op male patient on incentive spirometry. For those of you who don't know – this is a little plastic device you blow into. A plastic ball rises in a chamber, the height of which depends on the force of your expiration. One morning she went bopping into his room and said, "Mr. Smith, are you getting your little balls up?"

He replied, "Naw, I don't do that anymore."

That would be innocent enough, but the bed intercom was open to the nurses' station, and everyone at the station heard it. The laughter spread through the hospital and everyone's day was happier because of Mabel and her Erma Bombeck personality.

I love children, old folks, and dogs. I could write an entire book about funny things that children have said down through the years. Once a child came into my office and asked, "Are you Doctor Appointment?"

I had another small child to ask me, "Dr. Chambliss, did you born me?"

I remember a little black boy about three years old. When I went into the examining room to see him, he looked me right in the eye with his big eyes and said, "I hear you're a mean doctor!"

Once I did a nasal swab flu test on a three-year old who sternly said to me, "Don't ever do that to me again!"

One day in Burkesville they brought in two children, ages three and five, grandchildren of the local bootlegger. They had gotten into their grandfather's supply of liquor and helped themselves. I will never forget them staggering down the long hall in my office to the last examining room where the little five-year-old girl was helped up on the examining table and promptly passed out. I asked the little boy, "Did you drink your grandfather's whiskey?"

The reply was, "Uh-huh."

"How many times?"

He held up three fingers and said, "This many."

"Did your sister drink her grandfather's whiskey?"

"Uh-huh."

"How many times?"

"This many!" He held up all ten fingers. That explained her passing out. They made a quick recovery with no harm done. They were definitely the drunkest three- and five-year-old children I have ever seen. In fact, as far as I can recall, they are the only drunk pre-school children I have ever seen!

I remember another little three-year-old boy that I examined, and as I was leaving the exam room he said, "First you get me all naked and then you walk off and leave me." It has been a pleasure taking care of children.

A lot of my older patients think I am a bit too serious at times. They say things that will loosen me up. There was an 85-year-old lady who came in six weeks after she had an abdominal hysterectomy and when we were through with the exam she said, "Doctor, can I start having sex again?"

To which I said, "Well, I think that would be all right."

She said, "Well, it'd be the first time in thirty years if I did." She laughed really big, enjoying her clever entrapment of me.

One day an elderly gentleman had a cardiac arrest in my office, and we coded him and got him going. I called Bob Rhodes, the mortician at Trent-Dowell Funeral Home who operated our ambulance service at the time, to come and transport him over to the hospital. He had remained unconscious until we got him on the stretcher and on the way out he woke up and looked up and saw Bob Rhodes and then looked over at me and said, "Keep Bob Rhodes away from me!"

I remember on another occasion a lady came in saying that she didn't think her birth control pills were going to work. I asked why, to which she answered, "Because they keep falling out." Try keeping a straight face with that one.

Women will try almost anything to prevent pregnancy – except keeping the husband out of the bedroom. Especially before the birth control pill became available, they would try any kind of birth control they read about or heard about. One day a young lady, somewhat unsophisticated, came in and asked me to fit her with a diaphragm. She had heard about a diaphragm from a neighbor. I was examining her with the speculum locked in place when the nurse, Bea Mittag, stuck her head in the door of the examining room and told me there was an urgent emergency in the next room. I excused myself and the nurse in the room with me followed me out the door, unaware that I had not removed the speculum. Later she returned to the room and found the woman standing in the floor in a semi-crouching position with her legs spread wide apart – the speculum obviously still in place. She looked up and said to my nurse in a timid yet respectful tone of voice, "I don't think I'm going to like this kind of birth control." We had to take a break before continuing with the fitting of the diaphragm.

Another colleague tells about doing a pelvic exam and noting a peculiar grape- colored discharge. He asked the patient if she had noted the grape-colored discharge. She said, "Don't you remember? When you fitted me with a diaphragm for birth control, you said I could use any type jelly I wanted. I chose to use grape jelly." Of course, he was referring to one of the many spermicidal jellies from the pharmacy. After you practice medicine for a while, you learn to be very specific and not take anything for granted. You wouldn't believe what some patients can do with an aluminum-covered suppository without good instructions!

I have a similar story to the grape jelly story, but it is not printable. The funniest things I have ever seen or heard – I wouldn't print. They will be forever private!

Sometimes there is nothing you can do but laugh. When you fall down on the ice and bust your behind in front of spectators, what else can you do? What do you do when you are leaving someone's house and walk into the closet, rather than the outside door? You may never do that – but I can assure you that you will do something just as ridiculous someday. If you laugh with people, it always eases the embarrassment. It can, in fact, make an embarrassing situation fun.

Crying and laughter are two emotions we should never hold back, for our own well-being. We need them both to get through the world – believe me! We can cry and laugh by ourselves, but it is much better shared.

Laughter is good therapy for everyone. It contributes to a healthy immune system, and many "incurable" diseases have been cured by laughter. Physicians and psychologists are using laughter therapy more and more and are finding unbelievable benefits after all medications, surgery, and high-tech medicine have failed.

When you laugh, you are happy, and when you are happy, you are healthy. Studies suggest that the brain is more involved in physical health than had been previously thought. Laughter is "rewarded" in the form of increased protection from bacteria, viruses, and even cancer cells. Laughter has an effect on our immune system that causes an elevation in levels of a germ-fighting substance called immunoglobulin A. It increases our endorphin level, which makes us euphoric and relaxed – also enhancing our immune system. On the other hand, the absence of laughter or anger appears to trigger the production of aggression-related chemicals like adrenalin, which may in turn suppress immune system activity.

The mysteries of our immune system are gradually being unraveled, and there is good scientific evidence that not only laughter, but a positive mental attitude as well as an attitude of caring for other people gives our immune system a boost. A good sense of humor should be your constant companion and will be an invaluable asset for a life filled with good health and happiness.

One lady I read about tells this story. She had finally, after years, talked her mother into going to her Ob/Gyn doctor for a Pap smear. She exited the office saying, "I'm never going back to that doctor.

When he did my Pap smear and exam he said, 'My, you look spiffy today.'" Her daughter wondered why her doctor would say such a thing until she went into her mother's bathroom when they got home and found a can of Christmas glitter hair spray on the commode which her mother had used instead of her feminine hygiene spray. They both had a good laugh.

You never know what's coming next. In the course of taking a history from a single teenage girl I asked her a routine question: "Are you sexually active?" She replied, "Well, not every night!" Every night would be active, would it not? I went on to the next question with a professional face, but had an internal laugh!

There is also humor in the waiting room. One man had been waiting all morning while I delivered a baby at the hospital. He finally came to the window and said, "I may as well go home and die a natural death."

Another elderly man came in with a subconjunctival hemorrhage, which is a red eye caused from a ruptured capillary (small blood vessel) in the white of the eye. I assured him it required no treatment and would take care of itself. He came back to the receptionist's window, paid his bill with a check, and wrote on the check "For– *nothing.*"

My colleague, Dr. Sills, tells this story. He said, "I know sometimes we have to see patients quickly to get through the day, but an elderly lady at his office came back to the waiting room. Her husband asked, 'Have you seen the doctor?' She looked at the receptionist and asked, 'Have I seen the doctor?'" Dr. Sills said, "I didn't realize I was seeing patients that fast!" and laughed.

I will repeat myself. If you couldn't enjoy people and their uniqueness (God's creation) and laugh with them, you simply couldn't stand this profession for fifty-two years. The spouses of health care providers suspect and probably know that if we couldn't find some humor in what we do, we wouldn't be able to deal with the stress, the sadness, the tragedies, the terminal illnesses, and death every day. Kept in its right perspective, laughter is valuable to the health of the patient and the mental health of the physician and health care providers.

I'm sure God has a sense of humor. He gave Jimmy Durante a huge nose, and he made us all laugh with his self-deprecating humor. God must have said, "I'll put these jumbo ears on Bob Chambliss and see how he handles it." It's been fun!

CHAPTER 9

More Stories

I extracted these stories from presentations I made at the annual hospital Christmas parties. In fact, it was the hospital employees who first encouraged me to write a book.

You know, in the South, you can get away with saying anything about anyone if you add "Bless his (or her) heart!" You can talk about how ugly anyone is, how much weight they have gained, how bald they are, how bad they look--"Don't he look peaked [pale]? Just look how peaked he looks!" but you've got to say "Bless his heart!" "My goodness, he looks like he invented ugly! Bless his heart!" and "Have you talked to that woman he married? I think she is one brick shy of a load. Bless her heart!" and "Have you seen her baby? You know most babies are cute – but it can't help it! Bless its heart! God love it!" Now have you noticed Mr. Walz, our beloved hospital administrator. His head is getting as bald as a cue ball. Bless his heart! Look at Mr. Walz and all together now "Bless your heart!" Doesn't that make you feel better?

When I was born, it was told that someone looked at me and

said, "What a cute little boy, but didn't God work overtime on those ears? Bless his heart!" My big brother used to carry me around by my ears like a beagle pup, and I always thought this made my ears like they are. One day I was looking at my Grandmother Lyons and suddenly I noticed her ears. I said, "Grandma, your ears are as big as mine!"

She said, "Yes, they are. God made them that way. I like them that way and that's that!"

I said, "Okay." Grandma had no sense of humor.

I was presiding one time at the evening church service and got confused about the order of service. Our music director said, "Bless his heart." I replied that as I approached sixty-five, I noticed people said that to me more and more!

I heard someone say, "Dr. Chambliss is a good doctor, but he can't write worth a lick. Bless his heart!" It's true! One day a little six-year old boy was watching me write out a prescription and said, "We've got a little boy in our class who writes scribbly like that!"

"Dr. Chambliss can't hear it thunder. Bless his heart!" It is also true – hearing is one of my senses that isn't what it used to be and can be embarrassing at times. I have a really cute little eighty-nine-year-old patient who is one of my favorites. Recently my receptionist said her daughter was calling about her lab results. (I thought she said it was her daughter.) I went over each test and explained that they were all perfectly normal. The voice on the other end of the phone said, "Well, what's wrong?"

And I said, "Well, she's old and worn out."

The caller replied, "I think she is, too – this is she!" Bless her heart!

When I celebrated my sixty-fifth birthday I didn't feel or look sixty-five. I understand two people in housekeeping were talking one day and one said, "I think Dr. Chambliss wears a hair piece" to which the other one replied, "No, he doesn't! He could afford to buy one that looks better than that!"

You know I never let anyone use the word "old" in my office — only "older." You are only as old as you choose to act! I have raised three boys and often we have had as many as ten or twelve boys around our table, and I know that to them any mention of belching, farting, boogers, and cooties is the funniest thing in the whole world. Some of my stories are about on this level. Psychologists say that each one of us has a child locked up inside and that it is good to let the child come out from time to time. So, let's do it!

There are, however, some clear and definite signs to let you know that we are getting "older." I recently listed some of those ways.

You know you are getting older if you grunt every time you get up or sit down.

You know you are getting older if the barber asks you if you want him to trim your eyebrows. The first time Larry Collard asked me that I said, "Well, no," but now I let him do it.

There comes a time in a man's life when hair stops growing on his head, like Mr. Walz, bless his heart, and starts growing out the nose and ears. The ones growing out of your nose are like tree trunks and are attached to every nerve in your body, so you can't pluck them out like you women do your eyebrows. You pull on one of them and your leg jumps. Recently I got an advertisement for a nose hair clipper called a Turbo Groomer. It looked one step away from a miniature weed eater to me, so I didn't order it! I have more trust in my barber!

Speaking of unsolicited mail — you know you are getting older when you start receiving all kinds of advertisements for herbs and drugs and appliances for erectile dysfunction. The dreaded ED! All these advertisements say, "Do you suffer the heartbreak of erectile dysfunction? Fortunately, those who don't smoke, drink, or chew usually don't need them. I used to tell my male patients who drink and smoke that if they didn't stop they would die before they were sixty-five years old. They would give me a macho answer like, "Well, you have to go some time." Now I say, "If you don't stop drinking and smoking, there is a ninety-five percent chance by the time you are sixty-five you will 'suffer the heartbreak of erectile dysfunction.'" The response to that is "Really? I'll have to think about that."

You know you are getting older when you start receiving notification about Social Security and Medicare. I have my red, white, and blue card now, and I can go to the doctor any time I want. Last week, however, I received an advertisement wanting me to buy a burial policy. I have no interest in that!

You know you are getting older when clerks start giving you senior discounts without asking you.

You know you are getting older when the most important thing in your life is going to bed at 9:00.

You know you are getting older when you find yourself standing on the stairs and can't remember whether you are going up or down.

You know you are getting older when you start having youthful fantasies. I've always wanted a red Corvette convertible. Recently we were having dinner (southern for lunch) with the office staff and I told them that and I said, "I wonder what they would think at the hospital if I came driving up in a red Corvette convertible?" Dr. Williams said, "It would probably have two fence posts and wire stretchers hanging out the back." (He was making fun of my love for farming.)

You know you are getting older when other people start telling you to answer your own cell phone.

You know you are getting older when people start finishing your sentences.

You know you are getting older when you start comparing pains. Janet tells me how bad her ankle hurts, and then I tell her my knee hurts and you won't believe how my back hurts. She says, "Mine, too."

(Late addition from Mark Lowery.) "You know you are getting older when you have to decide – Do I want to cut my toenails, or do I want to breathe?"

You know you are getting older if you find yourself telling the same stories over and over and reminiscing a lot, and that's exactly what I seem to be doing!

Recently I started thinking, "What will people call me now that I am 'older'?" You hear people say, "That old coot." Webster defines coot as a fool. I don't want to be called that! I've heard old men called "old geezers." Webster defines that as an eccentric old man. I don't want to be called that! Old codger. Webster defines an old codger as a peculiar, odd, or curious old fellow. I don't want to be called that. We hear about grumpy old men. Janet says I am making really good progress with that one. I have heard men referred to as old farts. I'm beginning to understand that one with all these high-fiber healthy heart diets we doctors put heart patients on.

You hear men referred to as cute, little old men. I doubt if I qualify for that one. Bless my heart!

Recently Sharon Kennedy called me a "tough old bird." I like that better.

Finally, some men are referred to as grand old gentlemen. Maybe if I work hard at it, I can settle in there.

I am usually very serious and reserved and don't project my sense of humor. People have always said, "Dr. Chambliss, you are so calm and cool and collected and always under control. How do you do that?" Believe me, I am not always under control and the loudest my wife ever laughs is when I am not. She loves it when I am embarrassed, and it actually started on our wedding night. We arrived at a small motel, and the only room left was a room next to the innkeeper's quarters. The room was furnished with one of those tall beds that have box springs, mattress, and slats. We hadn't been in bed very long when the top end of the box springs crashed to the floor. Being sensitive to a possible embarrassment of my newlywed wife, I said something that I thought was calm and cool and reassuring, and it struck Janet as being very funny, and she laughed very loud and kept laughing

Let me tell you how loud Janet can laugh. We were at a motel in Louisville one night watching the movie *When Harry Met Sally* and Janet was laughing hysterically. A knock came at the door and some man said, "This is security. We've had complaints about the noise."

Janet said, "All we have in here is Diet Coke and popcorn, and we're watching a movie."

He said, "Well, please be a little quieter."

So I knew the innkeeper at the motel probably heard us, and I dreaded checking out the next morning thinking about what she might say. Something like, "Did you enjoy your night?" or something more catty, but she was nice and didn't say a word.

One night we were in New York City with another couple attending the old Jack Paar show. It wasn't over until one o'clock in the morning. I had needed to go to the restroom even before the show started, and by the time it was over I was really hurting – looking for the closest restroom. Unfortunately, when we came out of the theater they had already closed down the restroom in the lobby. When we got out on the street everything was closed down and now I was really hurting. I was afraid to go into an alley, afraid someone would kill me (a Kentucky boy's attitude about New York). I felt like one of these old men that comes into the emergency room with urinary retention who say to the nurses, "I don't care what you do to me, but do it quick!" Somehow I made it back to the hotel, walking very strangely, with Janet laughing at me the whole way.

Janet used to have arthritis in her hands and treated them by putting them down into hot melted paraffin, which would solidify around her hands when she took then out. She would keep it on until the paraffin cooled off. One night we got a call to go somewhere quickly, and Janet had this paraffin on her hands which had not cooled, and asked me to help her put on her panty hose. Only because I wanted her to hurry, I agreed. Most men have had some experience in helping their wife or significant other take her clothes off, but I dare say very few have ever helped her dress.

Well, you should have seen me putting on the panty hose. First of all, have you ever noticed that panty hose are only about this wide (6 inches) and your wife, (I'll have to be careful with this) is about this wide. Men have no experience gathering up those hose in their hands and doing those little release motions as you go up the leg. And then when you get one leg on – how do you get down to the other foot? Have you ever watched a woman put on panty hose? No, that's one thing women do that makes a man turn his head the other way. You see them go through some of the strangest motions and gyrations to get those hose on. I tried to put them on her, but the harder I tried the harder Janet would laugh. We were having so much fun we almost canceled our trip.

A few years ago in a Louisville restaurant, I walked into the wrong restroom. I encountered four or five ladies, said "Excuse me," and turned around and quickly exited the ladies' restroom with a red face. Janet was waiting on the far side of the room and some other woman said to her, "Did you see that man come out of the ladies restroom?"

Janet said, "Yes, that was my husband." She started laughing and laughed hysterically all the way out to the car. She loves it when I make a mistake. I can just imagine that woman telling her husband that night about the strange couple she met at the restaurant.

One afternoon at home I went strolling into the kitchen with only my shorts on and, unknown to me, Suellen Raley was sitting at the kitchen table with Janet. I made a quick exit. When Suellen left she said, "Nice seeing you, Dr. Chambliss." Janet laughed all afternoon about my embarrassment. So you see, I am not always under control.

I want to share with you some of the most extreme things I have seen and heard. I think you will enjoy them.

Recently at the Cloverport Clinic I ran into the worst gas problem I have ever heard of. A woman there told me she had gas so badly that when she passed gas it knocked her down to the floor. That made my morning and I laughed all the way back to Hardinsburg trying to visualize how this could happen. I wrote in her chart "serious gas problem."

And what about the worst discharge I have ever seen. This woman from SeRee came in and said, "Dr. Chambliss, I have a discharge so strong it burns holes in my underpants." I didn't take any chances. I put on two pair of examining gloves! I'm kidding about the two pairs of gloves, but you never know what you are going to hear next in a doctor's office.

Interesting underwear I have seen (in the examining room), and I've seen it all, from thongs to lace to push-up bras, to both women and men who wear none at all. The most interesting was worn by the thinnest patient I have ever had. It was a little old lady, eighty years old, also from SeRee, who weighed fifty-nine pounds.

I was examining her, and she had on little-girl training pants that had the day of the week embroidered on them. They were inscribed "Tuesday." It was actually Monday and as I observed I said, "Tuesday?" and she said, "Well, Monday's were dirty."

Little girls wear training panties inscribed Monday through Sunday, which is a reward for them to stay dry every day. I understand that! I don't understand training bras. What do you train them to do? I think it will take more than these little training bras to get them ready for a job at Hooters!

The most interesting names for private parts--everybody makes lists. The funniest list I have ever seen, except what men say to their wives when they want some loving, is a list of what people call their private parts. I thought I had heard them all but recently a woman came in telling me that "My dever hurts." I took a chance and got it right.

Dr. Williams was recently examining a little boy and as he started to take his pants down the little boy said, "Don't look at my Willie!" Dr. Williams has started his list.

Weakest male urinary stream I have ever heard of: You may or may not know – let me educate you again – that men as they get older have problems urinating because of an enlarging prostate. All of you who have changed little boys' diapers know they can spot you from fifteen feet if you are not ready to dodge. As the male gets older, it gets down to a dribble. We routinely ask the question when taking a history "Is your urinary stream as forceful as it used to be?" The reply made by my childhood barber was "Bobby, I can't pee over the end of my toes." Statements like that make for a lighter day, and I have enjoyed all of these colorful characters of the past.

Another prostate story. A sixty-year-old patient of mine married an eighty-year- old man and when she went into the bank the next week the banker teasingly asked her how her husband was holding up. Her reply: "Well, he's got a bad heart and a prostatuted gland." Now that's a serious gland problem!

It didn't happen to me, but I want to tell about a most remarkable recovery from a heart attack. A doctor had a patient who had almost died from a heart attack, but he made it through, and a year later at the hospital Christmas party the doctor saw him dancing and laughing and having the biggest time, looking like he had never been ill. The doctor said to him, "I see you have made a nice recovery from your heart attack. How did you do that?"

The patient said, "Well, you said get a hot mama and be cheerful."

The doctor said, "No, I said you have a heart murmur. Be careful!"

I love redneck jokes. Let me tell you my favorite one of the year. "You may be a redneck if you ever wanted to clean out your ears and couldn't find your truck keys."

CHAPTER 10

Interesting Stories from Cumberland County 1964-1969

SHOTGUN WEDDING

I hadn't been in Cumberland County very long when a fifteen-year-old girl from Pea Ridge was brought in because she had missed two or three periods. I confirmed the pregnancy by examination and a positive pregnancy test and told her parents that she was pregnant. Later on, I heard they had a "shotgun wedding" out on "the Ridge" uniting her and the reluctant boy in holy matrimony. There was a threat of using the shotgun if he tried to back out – which was what he was trying to do.

About two weeks later, the boy's father and brother came to my house looking for me one evening before I got home. My wife told them I was on the way home and to have a seat in the den. They said they would wait outside and backed their pick-up truck, complete with gun rack and two guns, into my driveway. When I arrived, they were sitting one on each front fender (trucks had front fenders back then) with their arms crossed and with a very somber serious demeanor (mad!).

I said, "Hello."

Their first words: "How come you said Jeb's daughter was pregnant when she weren't?" My mind went into high gear!

"Why do you ask?" I replied.

"Because she has 'come around' [a local description of menses]."

I replied, "Because I examined her and confirmed it with a pregnancy test."

"How can you tell if a woman is 'knocked up' by looking at her urine?" This was my description of the specimen – not theirs.)

This 15-year-old had a spontaneous abortion (miscarriage), which is very common, and they believed it was her menstrual period ("coming around").

I don't remember how I explained this to them, but it must have been an award- winning performance, because they eventually left, and I was unharmed! One thing I do remember is that from that time on if there was any possibility of a shotgun wedding, I wouldn't diagnose a pregnancy unless it was obvious to everyone in Cumberland County. Even today, when I pass a pick-up truck with a gun rack and guns, I think of it. This never came up in medical school!

THANK YOU, DOCTOR; I DIDN'T FEEL A THING!

One of my most memorable deliveries involved a sixteen-year-old from an adjacent county. She had recently been named Miss County Fair and was a stunning brunette – an absolute beauty!

The delivery was routine at first, with a saddle block anesthesia, which is what we used most of the time in the early part of my career. Epidural blocks had not yet come in vogue. We had no anesthetists. It was usually good and adequate anesthesia, but occasionally, even in the most skilled hands, would cause what was called a "high block" and not only anesthetize the perineal or pelvic areas, but would anesthetize everything up to the mid chest, which would paralyze the diaphragm, knock out breathing, and reduce the blood pressure to shock levels. It was usually easily taken care of by breathing for the patient with an Ambu bag and giving a vasopressor drug IV to keep the blood pressure up until the anesthesia wore off which usually took an hour or so.

I had delivered the baby and was starting to place the proper sutures in the episiotomy (incision) when the nurse informed me that the patient had no spontaneous breathing, no detectable blood pressure, and no palpable pulse! I told the nurse what IV drug to give, and by now she was in a panic mode when she told me the IV had come out. I said a quiet prayer.

I said, "Give me the syringe with the vasopressor drug," and I successfully injected it into the femoral vein in the groin area on the first attempt. My knowledge of anatomy, which I had learned so well at Vanderbilt Medical School, came into good use because there was no pulse to guide me and her peripheral veins were all collapsed.

I'll never forget this beautiful brunette teenager lying there deathly pale, motionless except for her expanding chest from the nurse forcing air into her lungs, no blood pressure, no pulse, and no IV. After I gave her the IV drug, her pulses slowly became palpable and her blood pressure slowly started to rise; she began breathing some on her own but still assisted by the Ambu bag, and her veins became distended enough to get an IV and proper meds going.

I returned to suturing the episiotomy and by the time I finished, she was waking up and what she said I'll remember until the day I die. "Thank you, Doctor; I didn't feel a thing."

I said, "Thank you for being a good patient, and thank God for being with us." She never felt a thing, but I died a thousand deaths. What if I had lost "Miss County Fair"? I think it would have altered my career forever. Thank God--He answers prayers.

MURDER AT FORREST COTTAGE

One night shortly after we had gone to sleep, the sheriff came to the house and told me that there had been a shooting out in the county in the Forrest Cottage neighborhood and he wanted me to go with him. Apparently the man had come home intoxicated and got into a fight with his wife. He ended up shooting her in the chest with a pistol. After he sobered up some, he said to her remorsefully, "I'm no damn good. Just shoot me!" He held the muzzle end of a shotgun to his mid sternum and handed the other end of the shotgun to her. She pulled the trigger and, of course, killed him instantly.

When I arrived, she was barely conscious but gave me this history. The man had a four-inch hole in his anterior chest and I could see his heart muscle through the opening. His heart had the entire right side blown away.

I gave my entire attention to the wife, who by this time was developing an acute tension pneumothorax. We didn't have time to get an ambulance, so we loaded her into the sheriff's car and called ahead to the emergency room to have a chest tube ready when we arrived. I had never placed a chest tube, but had helped do them at Louisville General. I immediately inserted the chest tube and placed the end of the tube under water as the instructions directed, and she was immediately relieved of the over-expanded chest which was collapsing her lung. We stabilized her and put her into an ambulance with a nurse at her side and headed her to the University of Kentucky Hospital in Lexington. She made the trip fine, survived the gunshot wound, and returned home within a week.

This took most of the night, and my wife recalls lying in bed thinking, *How am I going to raise these three boys by myself?* She was never happier to see me than when I came home at daybreak!

There would be many other occasions that caused her temporary distress. I don't think people realize a country doctor's wife is a significant part of the practice. She's been a partner with me every step of the way. Maybe she should write this book!

NEST OF BOYS

Most house calls I made were on geriatric patients who were bed-fast and had no way to get into the office or emergency room. I was happy to visit them, and usually the most significant thing about the house call was the "visiting." It usually made very little difference in the outcome of their medical problem, other than having a physician who took care of them come to see them. They liked talking to the "little new doctor." Some calls made all the difference in the world.

I was called to see an indigent family who lived at the edge of town back up in a "holler" in a one-room dirt-floor cabin. There was one bed in the center of the room near a wood-burning potbelly stove. It was mid-winter and bitter cold. In the bed were five little boys, ages one through five, with only their heads sticking out from under a dirty comforter. They were all coughing, and their breathing was labored. I threw back the cover and, much to my surprise, there were five little naked boys lying side by side burning hot with fever. They reminded me of a nest of baby mice. You can only appreciate this if you have ever uncovered a nest of little mice. When they are small, they are bright pink and have no fur.

All five boys had obvious pneumonia, so I gave each one a shot of penicillin and some prescriptions that were never filled. I placed a pan of water on top of the stove for a humidifier, and I said goodbye and informed them that I would be back the next day.

The next afternoon they were all better, and I gave them another shot of penicillin and repeated this five straight days, because I knew the injectable penicillin was all they were going to get. By the fifth day their chests were clearing and the cough and the fever subsiding. I had gathered up as many sample drugs as I could find at the office to complete their treatment. The last time I saw them, they were all running around the cabin, eager to see the doctor. I waved goodbye and never saw them again.

Thank God for penicillin. At least this drug predated my practice in the hills and hollers of Appalachia.

HE'S GOT THE ANXIETY

One house call I remember was at Leslie, Kentucky. An elderly man had been bedfast for twenty-plus years. His wife said they had taken him to every doctor within fifty miles and no one could find anything wrong with him. I examined him, and his exam was completely normal. His wife then said to me, "We have been told a lot of things, but I think what he has is the anxiety."

I said I agreed with her and recommended that she stop waiting on him and make him get out of the bed.

I was never asked to return.

MARROWBONE CREEK

Another house call remains in my memory. I was called to the Marrowbone community by a man who claimed to be in bed with pneumonia. He told me to come to Marrowbone and identified his lane. He said the road would run into Marrowbone Creek and you couldn't see the road on the other side. He directed me to turn right and drive up the flat rock bottom of the creek a hundred feet and then you could see the road turning left off the creek. He assured me the creek was only four to six inches deep and easy for any car to navigate. I followed his directions with some trepidation and plunged into the creek. I drove about a hundred feet uneventfully and, sure enough, there was a dry road going south. If that wasn't enough, when I got there I found a robust thirty-year-old man in bed with no more than an upper respiratory infection (bad cold).

I was beginning to have second thoughts about house calls but continued to make them because it was still in vogue in Cumberland County. By the time I moved back to Breckinridge County, Dr. Sills had already stopped making house calls, and I was happy. I have, however, throughout the years continued making a few house calls.

I especially remember seeing our elderly local funeral home director and my former Sunday School teacher, R.T. Dowell, monthly at his home. Routinely I would sit down by his recliner or bed, and he would pat me on the knee and say, "Bobby, you are a good little boy." He was one of my favorite Sunday School teachers and taught me a lot as a young teenager.

TRICYCLECTOMY

I was called out to the Leslie community in Cumberland County one day to rescue a little four-year-old that had ridden his tricycle off a wooden bridge and fallen six to eight feet into the shallow water of a small branch. The right-side pedal of his tricycle had been reattached by placing a nail into the hole near the end of the axle to hold the pedal on. The nail was bent so the nail wouldn't come out, and the pedal wouldn't come off. In the fall, the nail completely penetrated the little boy's foot, which was now firmly attached to the pedal. He was screaming with pain and wouldn't let anyone pick him or the tricycle up.

I had some Lidocaine local anesthesia in my medical bag, so I lowered myself off the bridge to the creek bed below with a loaded syringe and anesthetized his foot around where it was penetrated by the nail. I asked those standing by to find me a wire cutter and being farmers, they found exactly the tool I needed. I successfully, with the firm grip of a former cow milking farm boy, cut the head off the large nail, removed it from the axle and released his foot. I pulled the nail through his foot. He felt no pain.

I lifted him up to his momma, then the tricycle, and then lifted myself out of the ditch by holding onto the bridge, which was about an arm's length over my head. I was wet and dirty but happy to be of help to a four-year-old in distress.

You do what you have to do! Dr. Kincheloe, who was my childhood physician, allegedly did an appendectomy on a kitchen table in someone's home. I thought while driving back to Burkesville, *I probably will never do an appendectomy on a kitchen table in someone's home, but I did a tricyclectomy in a creek eight or ten feet below a bridge in Cumberland County.*

THE LAST OF THE COES
A PART OF HISTORY

One day at the office at Burkesville they carried an elderly man into my office and laid him on the examining table, barely conscious and too weak to walk. He was an African-American, short of stature, and had an unusual light yellow or bronze-toned skin (I later learned he was a cross-breed of Cherokee Indian, Negro, and slave-owning whites from the historic Coe town or Coe colony in Cumberland County). He was in moderate respiratory distress, and his chest was very congested. I was able with much help to stand him up and get an X-ray. His lungs were permeated by cancer, but of more interest was the presence of three .38 slugs and 70-plus buckshot from the distant past.

We didn't have a hospital at that time, so I sent him to Glasgow for hospitalization. I heard he died shortly after admission--the last of the Coes! Little did I know that I had become a part of history (like in the Last of the Mohicans) The man was Otley Coe, the last of the Coes from historic Coe town in Cumberland County.

Jack Baker, a Nashville radiologist, spent one month in my office as part of his medical school training at the University of Kentucky Medical School. The following are excerpts from a paper he wrote for his medical school professor along with a paper on Huntington's chorea entitled:

THE DEATH OF OTLEY COE AND
OTHER OBSERVATIONS OF A
CUMBERLAND COUNTY PHYSICIAN

Much of this information was obtained from a paper entitled
"The Coe Ridge Colony, A Racial Island Disappears" written by Lynn
Wood Montell of Western Kentucky University for the American
Anthropologist 1972, 74; 710/711 (on Google).

*On April 18, 1982, I had the opportunity to interview Dr.
Robert Chambliss of Hardinsburg, Kentucky. I was seeking information relevant to the accompanying paper. Dr. Chambliss had
been a general practitioner in Cumberland County from April 1964
through June 1969. Though he had not observed an abnormal
amount of Huntington's Chorea (common in Eastern Kentucky), his
recollections of those first years of his practice were too interesting not
to be recorded.*

*Dr. Chambliss' practice was centered in a single office in
Burkesville Courthouse Square. He had arrived fresh from medical
school to take over the practice formerly handled by two physicians.
As a result, he saw 80-120 patients per day for more than five years
he spent in Cumberland County. Dr. Chambliss estimated about
half of his fees were paid for by public assistance. He believes some of
the county's residents to be "third generation welfare people" who live
with a feeling of hopelessness and fatalism which inevitably leads to
depression.*

*Dr. Chambliss noted the number one problem in the county dur-
ing his stay to be alcoholism. The area was legally dry, but whiskey
(moonshine) was often made to supplement the unemployment com-
pensation that many of the men received. The largest single industry
was a sewing factory which employed mostly women. Dr. Chambliss
recalled that while the women worked, the men often ran errands*

and passed the time drinking. (They would take *her* to work in the morning and pick *her* up in the afternoon, and were thus called "go getters" (go get her). With regard to government handouts, Dr. Chambliss expressed his feelings that, "you can dump the entire United States Treasury into Eastern Kentucky and not solve the problems there."

The most interesting story related to me by Dr. Chambliss centered around Otley Coe, the last resident of Coe Town. Placed on Pee Ridge as a result of slave emancipation following the Civil War, the racial island known as Coe Town existed for ninety years as a "place of refuge for white women shunned by their own families and communities and as a breeding ground for a race of rather handsome mulattos, as a strong hold of moonshining and bootleggers, and as a battleground for feuds that produced a harrowing list of ambushes, street murders, stabbing and shootings. After years of raids, arrests, and skirmishes with federal agents and local lawmen, the Negroes' resistance was broken, and they departed the hill country enclave for the industrial centers north of the Ohio River.*

At the time Dr. Chambliss arrived in Burkesville there were only three Coes left living in the old ghost colony. Two of these left for Chicago leaving old Otley Coe as the last resident (though some of his descendants lived in Burkesville). One day Otley Coe, who was around seventy years old, stumbled into Dr. Chambliss' office. Dr. Chambliss recalled getting him onto an examining table and taking chest x-rays. The x-rays, when developed, showed Otley's lungs to be permeated with cancer. Though the cancer was the cause of death that day for the last Coe, it had not been the first intruder into his body. The x-ray showed what Dr. Chambliss described as 'three 38 slugs and more than 70 buckshot.' Otley Coe had obviously been a hard man to keep down!" (Montell, Lynn Wood, "The Coe Ridge Colony"; A Racial Island Disappears, American Anthropologist, 1972, 74; 710-711.)

THE RAWLEIGH MAN

I had a patient in Burkesville who had a very bad contact dermatitis of his hands. The skin was inflamed, tender, and cracking. He made several visits (maybe six) to my office, and I would give him various topical treatments, none of which helped. Finally, his visits stopped, and I didn't see him for over a year. The next time he came in I said, "I see the last ointment I gave you cleared up your hands."

He said, "No. The Rawleigh Man came to the house, and I got some Rawleigh salve that cleared it right up." Many things like this happened to keep this young doctor humble."

"Rawleigh men" peddled their Rawleigh products door to door years ago, and I loved it when they visited our home when I was a young child. I remember a product my mother always bought to make butterscotch pie, which I loved. The Rawleigh Man was already one of my heroes.

"DOCTOR, DO SOMETHING FOR MY BABY!"

The following was one of the saddest experiences I had in Cumberland County.

I was in the emergency room one day shortly after we opened the new Cumberland County Hospital. A lady came directly into the emergency room carrying her two-year-old toddler in her arms. She handed him to me and said, "Doctor, please do something for my baby!"

The two-year-old boy was obviously already dead--with fixed pupils, cyanotic, and cold. He had fallen in the yard on a wire sticking up out of the ground where an old rusty woven wire fence was embedded in the ground. The rusty wire sticking up out of the ground, approximately six inches long, had penetrated the inner corner of the child's right eye into his brain.

When the mother found him, he was motionless, with no respirations. I said to her with a lump in my throat, "No one can save your son. He is in heaven with God." I gently covered his limp, cold body with a blanket and hugged his mother and said simply, with tears in my eyes, "I'm sorry."

Driving home I thought about what Jesus did when similar tragedies were brought to Him. The Bible says, "He looked upon them with compassion." He had the power to heal, and He had the power to restore life, which on occasion He did, but that's not the main reason Jesus came to earth. He had a higher calling.

That day I became aware of my own compassion. It was intense! If I could have healed this child, I certainly would have. If I could have restored his life – I would have, but only Christ and His Heavenly Father could do this.

I thought a lot that day about what I can do. What is within my power? My conclusion:

- It is important to be compassionate and show love.
- I must spend my life learning all the medicine I can learn and acquire all the skills I can, so I can be in a position to help.
- I must make myself available – so I can do what I am capable of doing. The most intelligent physician alive or the most skillful surgeon alive is of no value to me and others when he is unavailable.

I have tried my best to do these three things from the start.

- Be compassionate (love my patients).
- Learn (all I can).
- Be available (all I can).

Years later, I am still trying to live by these three principles of my high calling, which started with the simple earnest plea of this Appalachian lady: "DOCTOR, PLEASE DO SOMETHING FOR MY BABY!:

Office: (270) 756-2258   Fax: (270) 756-1239
Res: (270) 756-2811   Cell: (270) 945-1624
Email: robertbdr@bellsouth.net

Robert B. Chambliss, M.D.
Family Practice Of Medicine

105 Fairgrounds Rd.   Office Hours
Hardinsburg, KY 40143   Mon. - Fri.
                                       8:00 am - 4:00 pm

Prescription For Staying Healthy

1. Don't Smoke
2. Walk or run 30 minutes three or four times a week.
3. Keep weight normal.
4. Eat mostly vegetables, fruits and cereals.
5. Sleep seven to eight hours each night.
6. Go to church.
7. Help your neighbors.
8. Laugh a lot.
9. Think you are going to be healthy.
10. Keep your dreams alive.

Robert B. Chambliss, M.D.

This is a copy of my business card, front and back, which emphasizes my availability. Each of my patients—the total is estimated to be around 5,000--have had access to all these telephone numbers all the years of my practice, which made me very accessible to the public day and night. On the back is my prescription for staying healthy. I had a print made of this, and it has hung in my waiting room all these years.

CHAPTER 11

Building a Practice

Every doctor is confronted with the task of building a practice. You first think of building a practice that will make maximum benefit of your skills and talents, and then, of course, you want to build a volume of patients that will make you financially successful.

But there is more to building a practice than numbers. I had the great fortune of never having to build a volume practice. I took over a practice of two young physicians who had just left Burkesville, Kentucky in Cumberland County, to return to specialty training, one in radiology and the other in anesthesia. It was common back then for young doctors to practice a few years after internship to pay off their medical school debt. This usually lasted three to five years, and then they would return to the specialty training of their choice.

Cumberland County had only one full time physician and was surrounded by medically underserved counties. From week number one I had more patients than I could say grace over even considering I was eager and willing to start work early and work into the night 24/7, including making house calls which was still common practice in Kentucky in 1964.

My practice in Cumberland County predates Medicare and Medicaid. When these two programs were started two or three years later, everyone wanted to go to the doctor and from then on it was standing room only. It was a gift from heaven (Washington and Frankfort). No more $3.00 for an office visit! No more $5.00 for a house call, and going to the hospital was as easy as checking into a motel. Many families put Grandma in the hospital while they went on vacation. There were many abuses of the programs, which had to be dealt with later with much pain and grumbling by the public.

Patients came in by entire families at one time. My fellow physician, Dr. Sills from Hardinsburg, always gave the same humorous reply when asked if he had been busy: "I saw two car loads from SeRee this morning," which you can appreciate only if you are familiar with this welfare pocket in Breckinridge County where many of the "local characters" live happily on welfare and going to the "Doc" was the highlight of the month.

I have always enjoyed sharing these patients from SeRee, as has Dr. Sills, laughing with them (never at them). Everyone in SeRee has a colorful nickname and they have all mastered the art of self-deprecating humor. I have learned a lot from them.

It wouldn't be unusual to see over 100 patients a day, most of them familiar, with minor or chronic problems requiring little of my time. Five and a half years later, when I returned to my hometown in Hardinsburg, Dr. Carroll James moved back to Indiana and handed his established practice over to me – also a high-volume practice.

Young doctors today think you are lying when you talk about seeing over 100 patients a day. You have to explain that it was a twenty-four-hour day – not 8:00-4:00 or 9:00-3:00. It included house calls, 10-20 emergency room calls, keeping the emergency room open 24/7, and nursing home visits on your "day off." There was always someone in labor, with babies delivered day and night – often at mealtime, family time, and church time. It also included 10-20 inpatients at the local hospital, which was not an uncommon inpatient census for one doctor thirty or forty years ago.

Because I knew I would need a broad knowledge of medicine and medical skills, I took extra training in those areas that I knew I needed. Unlike today's family practice physicians, I had excellent training in obstetrics, orthopedics, surgery, anesthesia, and trauma as well as general medicine.

I did obstetrics for the first seventeen years I was in practice. I thoroughly enjoyed it, and it was something I did well because of my training at UT Medical School and Louisville General Hospital.

Most family practice physicians in America have had to give up obstetrics because of the unfriendly medical malpractice climate, the increasing cost of malpractice insurance, and the lawyers and courts who said we had to measure up to the same standards of care as an obstetrician in Boston, or Louisville, or any large city. Of course, without a neonatal unit at our local rural hospital, neonatologists, anesthetists, fetal heart monitoring, and several other technologies, we couldn't do it.

I loved obstetrics and hated to give it up. I had excellent training in obstetrics, having delivered 60 babies as a fourth-year medical student and 200 babies as an intern at Louisville General Hospital. Added to my Cumberland County and Breckinridge County deliveries, this made approximately 2,500 total deliveries for my career.

Obstetrics is probably what I did best, and I definitely enjoyed it more than any other area of family practice. Confidence in my ability was boosted by the nurses I worked with. They asked me to do their deliveries and recommended me to their friends. I kept up with our local obstetric morbidity and mortality statistics through the years, and ours was equal to or better than the Louisville hospitals who had all the ancillary facilities and services. This was with a 5% C-section rate at Breckinridge Memorial Hospital compared to a 30-40% rate in the city. C-sections for convenience of daytime deliveries has never been acceptable to me.

So I gave up obstetrics first; then I gave up surgery and anesthesia after our outstanding and exceptional surgeon Dr. Earl Buchele's premature death. Emergency room trauma was gradually turned over to a new emergency room service our local hospital acquired, and orthopedics was reduced to simple non-displaced fracture care. After fifty years of providing in-hospital care, I also gave this up to younger doctors and hospitalists, so now my practice is reduced to office care only. (See Appendix A)

Only when I gave up my hospital practice in 2014 did I realize that seeing thirty patients from 8:00 to 4:00 could be a busy day, just as the younger doctors had attested to. We used to keep very brief records, but now the paperwork is astronomical. With the advent of EMR (Electronic Medical Records) we spend more time with papers and computers than we do with the patient. I have resisted all these changes and have always delegated everything I can, so I can spend as much face time as possible with the patients.

For forty-four years I had gotten up at 4:30 a.m., eaten breakfast at the hospital cafeteria at 6:00 a.m., made hospital rounds at 7:00 a.m., and hit the ground running at the office at 8:00 a.m., where my staff would have three examining rooms filled with patients waiting for me and several patients in the laboratory getting fasting blood tests.

We lock the doors at 12:00 noon for lunch and reopen at 1:00 p.m., and everyone in the county knows this is our routine. I go home for my wife's excellent big, home-cooked main meal of the day; then I take a thirty-minute nap and return to the office at 1:00 p.m. until we get through, with no definite closing time. It has been my policy down through the years to see every patient the day they need or want to be seen, and often we have to work past 4:00 p.m. Since electronic medical records (EMR) were initiated recently, this has changed dramatically the number of patients I can see and the amount of time I spend with those I see.

The people who work at the hospital and office and many of the public have said down through the years that they could set their clocks and watches by me – knowing my routine. Most of the time, no one would have to guess where I was. Having a routine, I should add, increases productivity. Most of the doctors I know who complain the most about being overworked are those that don't get to the office until 9:00, 10:00, or 11:00 a.m., and they stay behind all day.

I like patients who have a good attitude toward illness. These are folks who never think about getting sick. When they do get sick, they expect and are confident of a good outcome. In other words, their attitude is "We'll work it out," or "Let's do whatever it takes to fix it so I can get on with my life." It is a fact that those who think sick tend to stay sick, and those who think well tend to stay well. Through the years I have built a practice of these kinds of folks.

I used to feel badly when one of my favorite patients would suddenly disappear from the practice. I learned, however, that there are a thousand reasons for this, and I gradually adjusted to this common occurrence for all physicians. Politics, especially contentious school board politics, can cause a major realignment of patients. In the community and church, I remain cordial and friendly with them and will go out of my way to be nice to them. Some of them will return to the practice, and some have left and returned two or three times over the years. I ignore or minimize any reference to their absence.

One morning I was seeing a little boy in the emergency room and he kept saying, "We don't like Dr. Chambliss. Dr. Sills is our doctor," much to the embarrassment of his parents.

I said to the little boy, "But you like me, don't you?" to which he replied, "Yes, I really like you."

Practicing medicine in your hometown of 2,000 and home county of 23,000, taking care of your friends, neighbors, family, former teachers and classmates, patients of all ages, and all social and economic strata from the president of the bank to the welfare recipient can be a challenge. It's like practicing medicine in a fish bowl or arena, and everything you say and everything you do gets announced and evaluated on the telephone (which now includes smartphones), at the local restaurants, church, grocery stores, and Wal-Mart. You have to get used to it.

I hear things I am purported to have said about a patient's diagnosis or treatment and have often responded, "That sounds so stupid! I hope people don't believe I said that." Of course, we all know that all stories, after passing through ten or twelve people, take on some interesting changes. Most people are fair and take local gossip in stride, and most believe only the parts they want to believe anyway.

Some rural doctors worry and take offense at being misquoted and misjudged. Some physicians enjoy the attention and thrive on playing to the audience. Most of us take it all in stride and laugh at the comedy and enjoy the part we all contribute to life's stage. It was Shakespeare who said, "The whole world's a stage, and all the men and women merely players; they have their exits and their entrances, and one man in his time plays many parts." My main part as a health care provider has been satisfying, and I am convinced that the nine-year-old who said to himself, "I think I will be a doctor" made a good decision. Someone else has said that doctors have a front row seat to the entire panorama of life. From this front row seat, life has been very interesting and satisfying. Life has been good!

All physicians have three kinds of patients: 1) those who think you can do no wrong – almost God-like. 2) those who think you can do no right, and 3) those who think you are doing the best you can do under the circumstances. Fortunately, most people fall into the third group. They allow you to be wrong at times or say something in error or stupid at times. They realize that you are tired and overworked at times, crowded for time on some visits, unavailable at times and feel bad or sick at times.

You have to be kind and on guard with your critics, but there is more danger in treating the ones who think you can do no wrong. You can start taking them for granted, become less attentive, and work less hard at being that physician who won them over in the first place.

My "physician personality" enjoys a high-volume, problem-oriented practice which helps in a rural area where there are not enough physicians. I like to get patients in and out as quickly as possible, and get acutely and critically ill patients to the right hospital and the right specialist as quickly as possible at the least possible cost to the patient. Most of the physicians I refer to are the best in their fields, and most of them that I select are conservative and don't rush into surgery or expensive treatments that may not be necessary. Most of my patients know this and appreciate this.

Over the years, I have lost more patients for not spending as much time with them as they wanted than for any other reason. However, most people like to get in and out quickly, and they are the type of patients who have stayed with me through years. They understand that when the waiting room is full and people are standing in the hall and there is a high stack of charts of unseen patients on the half-door between the receptionist and the examining rooms, you have to take a history, examine, treat, and move on. The next time they come in and there are fewer patients waiting, I make it a point to "visit longer" and talk family, farming, basketball, or whatever I know the patient likes to talk about. They also know what turns me on – my three sons and nine grandchildren, the Kentucky Wildcats, church activities, gardening, and farming.

I try to balance out a five-minute visit with a fifteen-minute visit the next time. On one occasion the waiting room was empty, and a lady came in and started talking and kept on talking as we sat down. I thought I would see how long she would talk and never asked a question. This went on for 25-30 minutes. When she finally stood up to leave, I handed her the prescription I knew she had come in for.

I still hadn't said five words. Her final remark on exiting my office: "Dr. Chambliss, you have helped me more than any doctor I have ever gone to." I said, "Thank you." So I do understand the need for some people to talk and most of us do benefit from venting. We old docs, anyway, resent the computer taking away this important face time from our patients. The practice of medicine will never be the same with computers (electronic medical records).

The science and technology of practicing medicine has improved dramatically over the past fifty years. The art of practicing medicine now leaves a little bit to be desired.

Years ago, I made this printout that I wrote available to my practice. It discusses how a physician views himself:

YOUR FAMILY PHYSICIAN

The greatest honor anyone can give me as a physician is to say, "Dr. Chambliss is my family physician." It's like applause to a performer and definitely the ultimate compliment. To me it means you trust me to take care of your health needs and have faith that I will act in your best interests. It doesn't mean that I own you as a possession or that I can take you for granted. On the contrary, it means that I must have worked hard to have earned your trust and that I must continue to work hard to deserve your trust. I'm not sure that everyone realizes that a doctor works harder for those who give him their trust and confidence – but it is a fact.

When a physician senses that a patient doesn't trust him, he first will try to win their confidence; however, if the lack of trust continues, he will soon try to find another physician for them that may be more suited to their needs.

The physician/patient relationship is much like a marital relationship. They must be suited for each other. Sometimes the patient's and the physician's personalities are just not compatible. Fortunately, we live in a country where you, the patient, have the freedom to choose the physician that suits you. If he or she fails to satisfy your needs or expectations, you are free to choose another. I hope this system of medical care delivery will always exist in America.

A properly trained and competent family physician who is genuinely interested in you can take care of 90-plus percent of your medical needs. It is for certain that I don't know everything or have all the answers (beware of the physician that does), but if I can't take care of your particular problem, my objective is to see that you get to the right specialized physician for the proper specialized care at the proper time at the least possible cost to you.

Anytime I sense that you wish to see a specialist and would like a second opinion, I am usually quick to see that an appointment is made with the most competent specialist I know for your particular problem. Sometimes I am not aware that you feel this way, and I would encourage you to let me know. I do not take it personally or feel that you think any less of my ability. Taking care of you is such a big responsibility that I often appreciate having another physician's opinion and advice. I must, however, advise you that it can sometimes only add to your anxiety and confusion to have two or more opinions from an equal number of physicians.

I personally will try to treat you in a way that you will have confidence in what I say. You must know, however, that in this age of high-tech medicine I don't have all the answers. Many times each day I am asked questions I don't have an answer for. I learned a long time ago to answer with an honest "I don't know," but I can assure you that I will either find out, or if it is vital, refer you to someone who does have the answers. I don't intend to overwhelm you with some highly technical answer that means nothing to you or, in truth, to me.

Oftentimes in medicine it is more important to know what is *not* wrong than to definitely know what is wrong. Years of practice teach you when to probe further for an answer. A doctor who is unsure of himself or who has to turn over every stone can cost you a fortune in this high-tech age of medicine. A good family physician will always consider the cost of what he recommends – protecting your budget as well as protecting your health.

Like all athletes, and maybe like you, your family physician sometimes has a bad day. When I make a mistake or an oversight or don't have enough time to spend with you or when I'm just plain grumpy, I would like to think you can forgive me occasionally. 99% of the time I love what I am doing, and if I had to choose a career all over again, I would choose to be a rural physician. I love being your family physician.

I plan to continue to practice medicine as long as I can stay mentally alert and keep current with state-of-the-art medicine. When I do depart this office and this world, it will please me most for people to say, "Dr. Chambliss was not only my family physician – he was my friend." This is the kind of physician/patient relationship I enjoy most.

There are two quotations I have always kept visible since I have practiced medicine: "The first rule of every physician should be to love people" and "No one cares how much you know until they know how much you care."

There is another quote I have threatened to put on display in my waiting room: "I HAVE PREPARED FOR THIS DAY ALL OF MY LIFE."

I enjoy practicing medicine. I get great satisfaction out of helping people with their health care. I love and enjoy being a part of my patients' lives and families and doing what I can to make it better for them. I feel good when I can help them and humbled when they show their appreciation. This never changes with whatever system of health care delivery we have at any particular point in time.

I could tell a thousand stories about how gratifying my practice has been. One story comes to mind. This is a story about a pregnant teenage girl and her mother coming in to request a referral for an abortion. Everyone knows not to ask me to do an abortion. Of course, I advised against the abortion. I kindly explained that the baby had a right to live and would be the source of unknown joy and pleasure to them. I acknowledged to the mother that her daughter needed her love and support now more than ever. They reconsidered the abortion, and later I delivered a beautiful baby boy.

The mother was in the office approximately twenty years later with a female problem for which I recommended a hysterectomy. The mother said, "If you say I need this, I believe you. We followed your advice twenty years ago, and it turned out just as you said. My daughter has a fine son, and he is the light of our lives. We couldn't live without him. Just as you advised, my daughter went on to college and both my daughter and her son are employed and successful. They are both happy and well-adjusted and glad to be alive. Because of you – three generations of my family are happy with the outcome. Without you, we would never have known. I love you, Dr. Chambliss, then and now."

My answer: "I love you, then and now." Love is indeed supreme! We all make mistakes, and we all need love when we make those mistakes.

I have gone through the entire evolution of providing medical care from fee-for- service to Obama's attempt to establish a one-payer system and total socialized medicine. I don't like the direction we are now taking, but one thing I know for sure – there will always be sick people, and there will always be a need for health care providers. Physician-patient relationships will always be important.

I regret the recent decline in our medical delivery system, which amounts to poorer care at a greater, many times unaffordable cost. I will spend the rest of my days helping to repeal the Affordable Care Act – getting our system back on the right track.

But whatever system and delivery of medical care we have, the doctor-patient relationship should never change. The principles are the same:

Love your patients!
Help them if you can!
Do them no harm!
Accept the privilege of taking care of them as
<u>PAYMENT IN FULL</u>. (Fortunately, most of them pay.)

There is much more to being a physician than practicing medicine. You have to balance your life with your marriage, raising a family, hobbies, extra-curricular activities, church work, and recreation. The quality of medicine you practice is dependent on the success you have in all these areas of your life.

CHAPTER 12

Back Where I Belong

PART ONE – THE FAMILY FARM

I have often said Hardinsburg and similar rural mid-America towns are the last great places in the world to live, better yet, on a family farm. Much has been written and much has been romanticized about the family farm or the family ranch, but no one can fully appreciate it or feel it unless they have experienced it. Unfortunately, not everyone who is raised on a family farm "really feels it," but for those of us who do, there is a common bond and a common understanding with all those around the world who share this love.

Like my father, I am one of those who truly loves the farm. Despite the fact that I was the youngest son, he wanted me to have the farm because, as he said, "You are the one who loves it the most." He was right. I do love the farm. I feel a kinship and a spiritual bond to the good soil of this small Kentucky place where I was born and reared. It is both my mother and my child. If you admire her and praise her, I feel the pride of a parent. If you fail to appreciate her, I feel the hurt of a child. If I ever lost her, it would be as if I lost a member of my family. And so, I give her the respect and reverence I give my parents, and I give her the nurture, sustenance, and protection I give my children.

We give to her and she gives to us, and that's the way it's always been. Whenever she prospers – we prosper. Whenever she fails – we suffer. When used kindly – she is kind to us in return. This is nature's way! This is God's way, and farmers with no particular training in philosophy or theology seem to understand "God's way" more than most folks – because they live it and take part in it, and it becomes a way of life.

How do you tell anyone what the farm means to you? How can you understand the feelings of a boy grown tall? How do you follow the fiber of a man's mind as it weaves back through time to the mind of a boy?

It may start at a thousand points. It could start with twelve duck eggs. When I was nine years old, I decided I wanted some ducks. A neighbor promised me a dozen eggs in the spring, and when spring came she delivered the eggs. I watched the hen house daily for a hen who was "sitting" or ready to sit on any eggs provided for her to incubate with her body heat. After several days, I found my "sitting hen" and made a special box for her nest and placed her on my twelve duck eggs. I watched her daily, and it seemed an eternity for the incubation period to pass (I think it was twenty-one days.). I watched as the teeny ducks pecked their way out of their protective shells and was amazed that the old hen mothered them like her own "chicks." All twelve eggs hatched, and the little yellow fluffy balls quacked and waddled and squirted all over the chicken yard, then the barnyard, the pond and eventually the front porch. With all the protection the old hen and I could give them from dangers ranging from the rats in the hen house to the turtles in the farm pond, seven survived from ducklings to full-size ducks.

I was nine years old and ready for the fourth grade. Like most Kentucky boys, the greatest passion in my life was for basketball.

Nearly all of my friends owned a basketball, and I had to play with theirs or do without. Up to that point I had played with a smaller, cheaper ball. I very badly wanted a regulation-size basketball of my own, so I decided I would sell my ducks and buy a basketball. I told my mother my plan to sell the ducks, and she approved. I caught my seven ducks and tied their legs together with "binding twine" – three for one hand and four for the other. The problem was to find a way to transport them to Black Moore's Poultry House in Hardinsburg.

My seventeen-year-old brother had the family car for the Saturday afternoon and was going into town to pick up his friends. I asked him to take me and the ducks to the Poultry House. He said there was no way he was going to take me and seven messy ducks to town in a car he had just washed. So, like any nine-year-old boy, I told my mother, and she predictably make him take me.

My brother was mad, but reluctantly loaded me and the ducks into the back of the old Chevrolet and we headed for town. He drove to the center of town and stopped in front of the drugstore and bus stop near the courthouse – two blocks from the Poultry House – and told me to get out! I was horrified at the prospect of getting out on Main Street with two hands full of quacking ducks, with everybody laughing at me. I protested and refused to budge. After he was satisfied that I was crying enough and sorry enough to have inconvenienced him, he took me on around to the Poultry House and humiliated me further by telling Mr. Moore I was crying because I was selling my ducks.

Mr. Moore paid me $1 apiece for the ducks. With seven dollars in hand, I went directly home, got out the Sears, Roebuck catalog, and ordered the only basketball I could afford – the bottom of the line – for $6.95 and put my $7.00 plus postage in the mailbox.

There was an old basketball rim in the barn that could be repaired, so I got busy and repaired it. I found enough scrap lumber to build a backboard and attached the rim. I remember climbing up on top of the same chicken house where the ducks were hatched and, all by myself, using ropes to pull the heavy backboard up the side of the chicken house to a height where I could nail it to the side. The next week I bought a new net and attached it to the rim, and then I waited every day by the mailbox for the mailman to bring my new basketball.

After many days, it arrived. I remember it was a leather ball with a rubber bladder inside, and when inflated, it was out of round. As I played with it, a bulge on one side became more and more prominent, and it became harder and harder to dribble.

But I shot that irregular ball at that old repaired rim and rough lumber backboard a million times. My mother could look out of the kitchen window and watch her son playing on that dirt chicken yard all year long – in the hot summer sun, dodging the chickens – in the fall, with leaves all over the court – in the winter, after the snow was shoveled off – and in the spring, dribbling in the mud and the wind so strong at times it would blow a long shot off course.

She thought it was her son Bob, but in my mind, I was Bob Cousy of the Boston Celtics, lightning quick, dribbling easily around the helpless defender with a cross-over dribble, slipping the ball behind my back, giving a slight hesitation and then blowing by the next defender for an easy lay up. Or I was Ralph Beard standing at center court receiving the ball with one second to go and shooting his famous two-hand set shot from twenty feet and hitting nothing but the bottom of the net. I could hear the crowd going wild and running out on the floor and hoisting me to their shoulders and carrying me off the floor.

Or I would be the go-to guy in the critical part of the game. I would run out to the head of the circle and receive the pass, give a head fake to the left, dribble to the right, penetrating as far as I could until cut off by a second defender, give him a ball fake and get him up in the air, and then jump high over both defenders, hanging in the air and releasing the ball when coming down with a high arc just over the defender's outstretched hands and, of course, the ball would nestle softly in the net. In my mind I hit every last- second shot, made the impossible pass, and made the key defensive stop.

A picture of the University of Kentucky NCAA Championship team hung over my bed and I slept with my basketball every night. Like every Kentucky boy, I dreamed of playing for the University of Kentucky Wildcats, just like another Hardinsburg youth, Ralph Beard, had done. Ralph went on to become a three-year All-American at the University of Kentucky and one of its all-time greats. I never made the University of Kentucky basketball team. Very few Kentucky kids do realize this dream. I did, however, lead the Breckinridge County High School basketball team in scoring for three consecutive years, which all started with seven ducks and one little boy who was unashamed to dream big dreams on a little Kentucky farm.

How do you tell someone about a family farm? It could start at a thousand points. When I was ten years old, I wanted a 4-H project. I had seen Mr. J. S. G. Smart's registered Spotted Poland China hogs at the county fair, and they always won the grand championships. There were always purple rosettes hanging over his entries. So I asked my father to take me out to Mr. Smart's farm, and I selected a young gilt (female hog), the pick of the litter.

I brought it home and treated it like a queen with all the feed it wanted – later to learn, of course, this was a mistake. Time passed and the gilt matured into a beautiful animal – a little overweight, but beautiful, I thought. Mr. Smart had promised that I could return it to his farm and breed it to one of his prize-winning boars (male hog).

Loading and unloading proved to be a much greater task this time, but we did it twice – once to take it out to Mr. Smart's farm and another to go back and get her. Mr. Smart informed me about the gestation period, and we calculated the approximate date of delivery – the date my fortune would arrive. As time grew near in January, the weather grew colder and colder, and the day she showed signs of labor it was below zero.

I was up early that morning and watched her struggle and labor all morning long. It was freezing cold, and my breath froze around my nose and mouth, and my hands were blue. I would run to the house and warm up quickly and rush back so as not to miss the delivery of my prize-winning litter. About noon she had one of the biggest newborn pigs I had ever seen. I was excited! These were, indeed, going to be county fair champions. After she delivered the first pig and I had wiped it off and wrapped it up and placed it at feeding place number one, I settled back and waited for number two. She never struggled again, but I was sure she was just resting.

After three more hours and nearly frozen to death, I went for my father, who assessed the situation. He said, "I guess that's all she's going to have."

I was heartbroken. My prize-winning gilt couldn't possibly have just one pig! "How could that be?" I asked my dad.

"I don't know," he said. "It just happens sometimes, but nature has a way of averaging things out. She may have fifteen the next time." He never mentioned until later that it's a good practice not to get breeding stock too fat.

Things just happen sometimes – a good lesson for a young boy. I say that now as a physician. My patients ask, "Doctor, why did that happen?"

"I don't know. Things just happen sometimes."

I eventually learned an even greater lesson in life – "It's not what happens that measures your worth – it's how you react to what happens."

We eventually had a good laugh about my one-pig-producing champion sow. The most valuable thing to come out of that experience, however, has nothing to do with hogs. I got to know Mr. J. S. G. Smart, whom I now consider one of my mentors. Last year I called him on his 100th birthday to congratulate him. He was appreciative, cheerful, and talkative, as usual. "I put up grape juice today, enough for two years," he said with a chuckle. At age 100 he lives alone and independently – still gardens and farms a little, drives his pick-up anywhere he wants to go and never misses church. His positive mental attitude and joy for life rival Norman Vincent Peale's; his faith in people, his community, and America rival Ronald Reagan's. Mr. Smart is Mr. Positive Mental Attitude. Life has been a joy to him and his life a joy to everyone he knows.

I have told many people and I've told Mr. Smart himself that I want to be just like him when I'm 100. I'm trying my best to emulate his life – which has been an inspiration to all Breckinridge County. I thank God often for Mr. Smart. Once he told me, "Doctor Chambliss, I pray for you often." Wow! I say "wow" because I believe the Bible scripture that says, "The earnest prayer of a righteous man has great power and wonderful results." (The Living Bible). With my mother and Mr. Smart praying for me, how can I go wrong?

How do you tell someone about a family farm? It could start at a thousand points. It could start with a little boy who always wanted to make some money on his own, and a father who could understand this. So my father said, "Bob, if you want to make some money, then gather up all the bottom leaves that brown up and fall off the tobacco before we harvest it." Some of the bottom leaves on a tobacco stalk mature and fall off before the tobacco is cut and housed in the tobacco barn. These leaves (called prime leaves or trash leaves) were dry and brittle, and if you saved them you had to get up early in the morning when the dew was on and the leaves were moist and pliable. (We called it "in order.")

You would have to crawl on your hands and knees under the five-foot-tall tobacco plants, which were wet with cold dew. The leaves overlapped the rows, blocking out all the morning sun. The cold dew soaked your clothes, and the coldness penetrated your flesh to the bone, it seemed. When you emerged from the end of the first row with your arms full of tobacco leaves, you were shivering, and your wet hands would be shriveled up like a prune. But to get your leaves and the money you knew they would bring, you turned back up the next row and down another and continued until the morning sun began to dry the leaves, making it impossible to get more.

Then off to the tobacco barn to tie up the leaves, looping a string around the stems of three leaves on one side and three on the other in a continuous fashion until the four-foot-long sticks were full of hanging leaves. The tobacco stick loaded with leaves was then hung up in the tobacco barn for the stem of the leaf to fully dry. After three or four weeks, when fully dry, the leaves were tied up in "hands" composed of 15-20 leaves and again hung on a tobacco stick ready to be taken to market.

I worked hard at this for weeks, it seemed, and waited for the tobacco to be taken to Louisville for the first market after Christmas. My leaves brought $129, which I thought was a fortune, the first money I ever earned.

With that money I paid $100 for a club calf, which I raised and eventually sold for $385. With that money I bought two club calves the following year and invested the balance in government bonds, at that time called "War Bonds."

From that starting point, there was an endless succession of bigger and bigger 4-H and FFA projects with bigger profits and more "War Bonds." When I entered the University of Kentucky as a freshman there was $5,000 in mature and maturing bonds which, along with part-time jobs and scholarships, paid for my first three years of college, after which I entered Vanderbilt University School of Medicine with a new bride – flat broke, but determined to become a physician.

The family farm had provided one enterprising little boy with the opportunity to earn money from his own efforts and had introduced him to the free enterprise system. It created in him good work habits and a desire to improve – to succeed and to excel – to be all that he could be.

How do you tell anyone about the family farm? The farm is a big part of my earliest memories. As I remember it coming out of the Depression – there were gullies on the farm deep enough to drive a team of horses and wagon in, an indictment of the previous generation, which had been more exploiter than nurturer. The large frame house was unpainted and in need of much repair. Chickens "dusted" in large holes of dust under the trees, in the back yard, and around the house because there was no fence between the chicken yard and the house yard. There were fences around the pastures, of course, and around the garden spot to keep the chickens out of the garden. There was no grass on the yard from the back porch to the outdoor toilet. To keep out of the mud when going to the toilet, stones had been placed at adult step intervals. As a young child, I had to jump from stone to stone.

I noticed that my friends in town had nice yards, some with picket fences. We had numerous aunts and uncles on farms around Breckinridge County, and when we visited, I noticed their nice yards and fenced-in chicken yards. I wanted that for our farm, so I asked my dad to buy the wire, and my first home improvement project was to fence in the chickens and seed the yard with grass, eliminating the "dusting holes" under the trees in the yard. I have been steadily improving the farm ever since.

I always liked pretty fences, and from that day to this I have been improving the fences on our farm. When I bought the farm after entering medical practice, one of the first things I did was to tear down the old line fences around the two-and-a-half-mile periphery of the farm and replace them with sawed cedar posts from Cumberland County painted white and aluminum coated woven wire fences. After a few years, these all came down and have now been replaced with four plank board fences – Bluegrass horse farm style.

I still do most of the repair and maintenance on these fences myself, on my day off and after office hours. Most of the interior fences on the farm I have built by myself. I get great satisfaction from these picturesque fences and improved pastures grazed by prize-winning Hereford cows. Mowing out fence rows and clipping pastures is one of my favorite pastimes and relaxes me in a way that only other afterhours farmers can appreciate.

While mowing the fields seated on my tractor, which our sons jokingly refer to as my "throne," I get great satisfaction remembering what the farm used to look like and take pride in the improvement that has been made from my own labor – my own sweat and blistered hands. Every post, every board, every gate, every square foot of the 120-acre farm has my fingerprints and footprints and sweat on it. This is what makes a family farm. It does in fact become a part of you. You become intimate with every square foot of land because you have been over it a thousand times by foot or with a hoe or a plow or disk or harrow or planter or combine or baler or tractor or truck.

You know every rock, every wet spot, every bush, and every stump. You know every shrub and every tree, because you planted most of them. You know where every ditch was, and you remember the years of filling them with rocks and trash and old fence posts and brush. You remember the bulldozing, the damming, the water diversion, and the seeding that it took to "heal up," as my dad said, the deep gullies eventually blending them in with the pasture.

You know all of the "poor spots" where the soil is thin, and you remember the years of trying to build up the soil on these spots with barn manure, tobacco stalks, lime, and fertilizer. You know all of the choice spots on the farm for a tobacco patch, or pickle patch, or a watermelon, strawberry, pepper, tomato, or garden spot.

You know which fields are best for corn, which are best for soybeans, which are best for wheat, and which ones are best left in pasture. You learn how to rotate the crops from corn or beans to wheat with grass and nitrogen-fixing legumes and then to pasture for two or three years and start all over again. You learn the proper principles of agriculture diversity and the principles of mixed husbandry of animals and plants. As temporary custodian, you learn that it is the responsibility and moral obligation of the producer and consumer to return to the soil the energy you extract from it and to protect it from erosion.

You know the nature of the soil and you know the fields that are too wet for April planting but are best seeded in late May or early June. You know the pH of the soil and when it was last limed. You know the last soil analysis, and you know each field's production history for as far back as you can remember. Through the years, you learn both the art and the science of handling the soil.

You know what the farm looks like in the spring and the summer and the fall and the winter. You know what it looks like covered with snow and six-foot snow drifts. You know what it looks like after six weeks of solid rain when you can hardly walk in knee- high boots. You remember how disappointed you were with how it looked after two months of no rain in mid-summer. But you also remember how it looks when the rain has been plentiful and the pastures are lush and the corn is over your head, with fat cows grazing in well-groomed pastures surrounded by well-kept fence rows.

You remember where the woods used to be and how your father cut the timber to build the barns when you were a kid. You remember the old sawmill that sat in the edge of the woods. After cutting the timber, you remember cleaning off the land and burning the brush piles, and you remember the many years it took to bulldoze the stumps out and for the others to rot and be removed. Not a trace remains now, but the woods still lives in your memory because you played there and gathered hickory nuts and mulberries there, and hunted squirrels and coons there, and spent hour after hour climbing trees or lying on your back watching the sun as it filtered down through the leaves of the tall trees.

You remember your father building all the farm ponds, locating them in the lowest wet spots not suited for cultivation. You remember that a farm pond to a farm boy is not only a source of water for livestock but the source of recreation – swimming in the summer, ice skating in the winter, frog gigging in the fall, and fishing all year round.

You remember killing hogs in the winter, grinding sausage, curing hams, canning sausage and tenderloin chunks, and rendering lard. After rendering the lard, you remember taking the rinds and making soap. You remember the summer garden and helping your mother can hundreds of cans of corn and beans and tomatoes, blackberries, peaches, pears, mincemeat, apple butter, jam and grape jelly. You remember laying out peach halves in the sun on newspapers on the galvanized metal roof for the sun to dry. You remember filling the cellar with potatoes and apples. You remember gathering bushels and bushels of hickory nuts and walnuts.

You remember the extra money your mom used to get from eggs, butter, and cream which she took to the Mattingly's grocery on Saturday afternoon and exchanged for other items – a good barter system long since stopped because it was considered unsanitary by the government agencies that now favor "big agriculture."

You remember the watermelon patches and the huge family reunions every summer where everyone brought food and placed it on three farm wagons lined up end to end. There was always enough food to feed an army. Everyone ate until they were nearly sick, and there was still much food to be taken home.

You remember the wheat thresher in the spring, and the corn shredder in the fall, and how exciting it was to have all the farmers in the neighborhood on your farm helping bring in the crop, along with the gigantic meals your mother had to fix to feed all the workers.

You remember the little club calf that you first took to the county fair, which stood last in its class. You remember trying each year to improve and finally winning the big prize. You remember your children improving their livestock until they were able to take championships at county fairs all over the state and win some national honors.

You always remember living with the weather and being at its mercy. You remember the good times and the bad, the disappointments, and the ever-present expectation of better times. You remember the hours and hours you spent in the fields alone with a hoe or on a tractor, which provided for excellent "thinking time" when you worked out your dreams, your values, and your philosophies. Farmers always have plenty of time to think about life and family, God and country.

You are constantly exposed to nature (God's creation). You constantly witness the miracle of renewed life, which Sir Albert Howard described as the "Wheel of Life" starting with birth – growth – maturity – death and decay from which new life arises starting the cycle all over again. You understand, as Wendall Berry writes in *The Unsettling of America*, "nothing that dies is dead for long – that the land moves in and out of our bodies and our bodies in and out of the land." He further explains, "The soil is the great connector of lives – the source and destination of all." He is right! You walk through the same fields your father walked through and the same fields your children and grandchildren will walk through – the soil connecting the past and the future as surely as does our genes and DNA. I recently saw Disney's great movie *The Lion King*, which wonderfully presents this "Circle of Life."

Witnessing these ever-changing forms of life's cycle makes the theological concepts of spiritual rebirth and life after death easy for the "people of the soil" to understand. In fact, all of Christ's teachings, such as the parable of the lost sheep or the parable of the sower, are easy for a farmer to understand. A tree is known by its fruit! You do reap what you sow!

You do feel a kinship and spiritual bond to the soil, because the farm sustains you both physically and spiritually. You give to it, and it gives to you. You fight for its existence, and it fights for yours. You listen to it, and it listens to you.

I will never forget when both my father and later my mother died, and I was overcome with grief. I left the house and walked in the fields and cried out loud where no one could hear me but God and the fields and the cows. The same fields that had received my sweat also received my tears. And when my grief was fully released, I returned to the house to my eight brothers and sisters, and we reminisced about the good times and the happy times our family had shared on the family farm.

The traditional family farm is the backbone of America. I regret the passing of the small family farm. I agree with Wendall Berry, renowned Kentucky philosopher and poet, who writes, "The care of the earth is our most ancient and most worthy and after all our most pleasing responsibility. To cherish what remains of it and foster its renewal is our only legitimate hope."

I practice medicine for a living. But every year I work hundreds of hours on the family farm, and every year I spend considerably more on the farm than the farm returns. But the return I get from the family farm cannot be measured in dollars. You can measure it only in pride, contentment, and peace of mind. We raised our three sons here on the family farm, and the values they learned here are priceless. They are what I want my boys to live by and carry on to the next generation.

Chambliss Farm

Chambliss Farm

A - First House
B - Second House
C - Birthplace
D - Robbins Truck Line
E - Fairgrounds

Our dream house 1979

My hobby

CHAPTER 13

Back Where I Belong

PART TWO: BRECKINRIDGE COUNTY

Except for the time I was in college and medical school for six years and three months and serving the wonderful people of Cumberland County for five years and two months (where I got my real training), I have had the good fortune of living in Breckinridge County on the Chambliss family farm – *where I belong.*

My medical practice in Breckinridge County has been exciting and interesting from the first day. I was accepted and shown love and local pride from the start. The home folks' love and acceptance has made me work hard to deserve it. I have never questioned or regretted my choice.

On the very first day, I got a most interesting referral from three generations back. An elderly couple in their eighties came in and related to me that they had been taught by my father's older sisters in a one-room elementary school near Falls of Rough in rural Breckinridge County in the early 1900s (1900-1915). They related to me without reservation that the Chamblisses of Falls of Rough were the smartest family in Breckinridge County; therefore, I most assuredly would be a smart doctor. They asked me to be their family doctor that day. Imagine that! They may have meant the most educated family, but *smart* sounded good to me. Family loyalties are strong in rural America.

All four of my father's older sisters were teachers in the rural Breckinridge County School System. Dad once told me that every morning they would get up early, saddle up their horses, and ride off in different directions to a rural school, each of which maintained a stable and water supply. The older, bigger boys at the schools would meet them, put the horses in the stables and feed and water them before school "took up."

Eventually they all married well and left Breckinridge County. One of them, Zilpha, married Styles Howard of the Breckinridge County, Glen Dean, Kentucky, Howard family. Styles was a college professor at Clemson Agriculture College of South Carolina. He taught electrical engineering. This opened the door for a very rare college education for the Chambliss brothers: Henry, Paul (my father), and Vernon (three out of four.) The fourth son, Herb, had cerebral palsy.

Very few rural people in the early 1900s had the opportunity to get a college education. Each fall, the brothers would ride a train to South Carolina and return after the spring term was over. They would live with their childless sister, Zilpah, and her generous husband, Professor Styles Howard, at very little cost to them.

They all enrolled in the College of Engineering with both my Uncle Henry and my father earning a degree in electrical engineering. Uncle Henry graduated in 1917 and eventually became President of the Montana Power and Water Co. My dad graduated in 1919 and took a job with an electrical company, Robbins and Myers Co., in Springfield, Ohio.

My parents, who married while Dad was still in college, started their family of eleven while in Ohio, and my father eventually decided that a city was no place to raise children. His love for the farm and working outdoors lured him back to Breckinridge County where they farmed, taught, and eventually started a farm supply store operated as an independent agency of Southern States Cooperative out of Richmond, Virginia. He and my brother Jack eventually sold their business back to the co-op. Dad did whatever else he could to raise nine surviving children. He was the hardest worker I have ever known.

My Uncle Vernon, after two years of college, returned to the Chambliss farm, which had been moved from Falls of Rough to Hardinsburg after my grandfather William Henry Chambliss, a school teacher and farmer, died at age forty-nine of tuberculosis.

For years my grandfather recorded all the deeds and mortgages, etc. at the courthouse in a beautiful English script. Following in his footsteps, my father and eight brothers and sisters also had beautiful penmanship. My penmanship from the start has been barely legible, which probably destined me to become a physician. I missed out on that gene!

That about exhausts my knowledge of the genealogy of the Chambliss family. I do know that the family ancestors were French Huguenots who first came to America in the 17th century. The name then was Chamble, later changed to Chambliss. They migrated to South Carolina and then to Falls of Rough, Kentucky, in Breckinridge County.

Hardinsburg is a friendly town where everyone knows your name and everyone cares for each other. They rally to help anyone in need and grieve with each other's losses or trouble. They celebrate your successes. We all laugh with each other about our individual unique qualities or peculiarities. You can get by with saying almost anything about anyone if you add "Bless your heart."

We have always had more than our share of "town characters" whom everyone enjoys. Everyone accepts you as you are. Almost all Breckinridge Countians believe in God and most are churchgoers--some regularly, others only on Easter and Christmas. Most of our citizens are conservative in nature and philosophy despite their political party affiliation. Most love basketball with the University of Kentucky and the "Big Blue Nation" being the most vocal. The University of Louisville fans, not to be outdone, are also very vocal.

Returning to Hardinsburg in 1969 after a twelve-year absence for education, I was ready to take my place in this small rural county-seat town. When I left Hardinsburg, there was a sign on each side of town which read Hardinsburg, population 900. Today it is about 2,300 with 20,000 in Breckinridge County. Everyone seemed happy I had chosen to return home, and I have been happy here.

Despite our small population, the Breckinridge County High School has won two State Basketball Championships, 1965 and 1995, a source of great local pride. Hardinsburg has produced two All-American Basketball players, both named Beard, one African-American and one Caucasian. Ralph Beard was a three time All-American at the University of Kentucky and National Player of the Year for two years. Butch Beard was All-American at the University of Louisville.

Our school system is excellent, and there are families in Breckinridge County who year after year produce children with above-average academic achievements. We have graduated students from many of the finest universities in America, from Harvard in the East to Berkeley in the West.

Regrettably, we lose our children to the large cities because we are rural, with very little industry. Our loss is America's gain! We are very proud of our students.

Crime and drug abuse have been traditionally low in Breckinridge County. Recently and regrettably, drug abuse has increased dramatically, a significant problem for all physicians. Not only does everyone know your name, they know your lifestyle. So, if you don't want to be the talk of the town – you had best play it straight. I have been fortunate to live in such a community, which has been a good place to raise our three sons.

Bryan, our oldest, is a Harvard-trained psychiatrist and, until recently, an Associate Professor of Psychiatry at Drexel Medical School in Philadelphia.

Jim, our second son, graduated from the Denver School of Law and practiced in Vail, Colorado, and Kentucky for ten years. After sustaining an incapacitating closed head injury in a motor vehicle accident, he changed his direction to research and recently received his PhD in Art and Medicine from Melbourne University in Australia. He has done extensive research on the effect of epilepsy on artistic creativity, which has received international recognition.

Brad, our third son, has a successful mortgage company in Elizabethtown, Kentucky. He served as National Vice President of the Future Farmers of America and currently has a nationally recognized herd of registered Hereford cattle.

Of course, as a proud father, I will write more about my sons in an upcoming chapter.

There are hundreds of Breckinridge County students with equal accomplishments. I am proud of all of them, but especially the ones I delivered and to whom I was their family physician. They are all like my own children.

Breckinridge County, I am happy to say, is one of Kentucky's top agricultural counties. Beautiful Rough River Lake is located between Breckinridge County and Grayson County and is an outstanding recreational area that annually attracts thousands of people from Louisville and southern Ohio.

The citizens of Breckinridge County represent the entire social spectrum. On any given day I may see a bank president, a welfare recipient, a member of a minority, a migrant worker, a Mennonite, a high academic achiever, a handicapped person, an athlete, a farmer, a school teacher, a mentally retarded person, a minister, and the list goes on and on, covering the entire spectrum of humanity.

They may have good health insurance, Medicaid, Medicare, or no insurance at all. Many have no ability to pay for their medical care. I treat them all, with or without the ability to pay. Physicians are privileged to have a front row seat to the panorama of human life, and Breckinridge County provides that entire spectrum.

This panorama of different people has a variety of problems. Google says there are 30,000 human diseases known to medicine. On any given day I may see a patient with a common cold, a laceration, a urinary tract infection, a gallbladder attack, a sinus infection, a broken arm, a bee sting, a heart attack, poison ivy, bronchitis, an abscess, appendicitis, pregnancy care, or strep throat, just to name a few. Some I have no idea what's wrong with them. Some need a routine visit for hypertension, diabetes, etc. Some need an annual examination, employment physical or truck driver examination, or treatment for any of the 5,000 common and uncommon diseases a physician sees, some of them daily, some once in a career.

I once had a dream of a long line of sick people reaching into the sky, reaching into infinity. I was methodically going from one to another- to another – to another. In fact, to date, after fifty-three years of practice and approximately 700,000 patient contacts, I'm still moving up that line. Take note – I said *up*!

I have always enjoyed the variety of family practice, and when I go to work every day, I have no idea what I will see next. That's what I love most about it. Every minute of every day is a new adventure, a new contact, a new experience, a new challenge, a new opportunity to practice my arts and skills, and a new challenge to bring something to the surface I learned years ago.

As a physician, I have always tried to treat everyone with equal respect. We have tried to see every patient the day they need to be seen or even the day they want to be seen. If it turns out to be a 40-patient day or 140-patient day, like during a flu epidemic, we simply work faster and stay later. We do this by scheduling an appointment every 15 minutes and work in all walk-ins without appointments as soon as we can. These numbers are not as high now since the practice was sold to the local hospital in 2011, and some things have changed. In recent years, we have added four nurse practitioners to the county medical staff, including two in my office and one each in outlying clinics around the county. We have eight physicians (including a surgeon, a pediatrician, and a psychiatrist.)

As a young physician, I was very much opposed to physician assistants and nurse practitioners. In time, I became so overworked that twenty-three years ago I added a male physician assistant, which didn't work out too well, and he left. I continued to take care of all the work load by myself! Seventeen years ago, I had the opportunity to add a female nurse practitioner to the office staff who completely changed my mind about nurse practitioners and physician assistants. Marinetta Van Lahr, who had previous experience in nursing and later in home health care, is a native of Breckinridge County and the wife of a local pharmacist. She later took her training as a nurse practitioner and had some experience in a physician's office in a nearby town before coming to our office.

She was a mature nurse and always a brilliant student before she decided to go back to school and become a nurse practitioner. She has good Breckinridge County common sense and I trust her with my patients – even my family. My patients love her, trust her, and respect her. I have turned most of my well-woman exams over to Marinetta. These are time-consuming if done well, and many women, I think, prefer a woman doing their pelvic and breast exams and talking to them about the things unique to women. She stays up to date on all female-related problems, and I often consult with her. As I've said, I have never been intimidated by someone who knows more than I do, male or female.

My change in attitude toward nurse practitioners came just in time. We are in the midst of a major change in the delivery of medical care in America. There is a major shortage of family practice physicians; nurse practitioners are replacing "country doctors" and will be America's first line of medical care in the future, especially in rural areas. There are very few of us physicians left who were trained as "country doctors."

I have been in solo practice most of the fifty-three years that I have practiced medicine. On two occasions I have added a partner. The first one, Dr. Bernard Dailey, who married into a prominent Breckinridge County family, joined me and after a couple of years decided to open his own office.

The second was supposed to be the ideal replacement for me eventually in the person of Patrick Williams, M.D., a local boy and also the son of a local pharmacist, who married my niece's daughter. I had delivered both of them as babies and was their family doctor. I waited many years for him to get through school and join my practice and eventually replace me.

Patrick is a brilliant student who had specialized in internal medicine, and he was liked by all. I think he was disappointed or disillusioned by the disproportionate number of patients that he had to see with common colds and minor things that were totally unchallenging to the skills he had acquired in internal medicine. He eventually opted to become a hospitalist in a large city hospital where he "would be more challenged." (my opinion). He was recently voted a "TOP DOC" in Louisville.

I may add that all doctors get tired or bored with treating the more common and mundane problems that present in a family practice. But here is the way I look at this situation: the patient who comes in with a simple problem that is annoying to him is a friend of mine to whom I can give some relief, and it gives me the opportunity for a short visit. The next visit, unfortunately for the patient, may be more challenging. Also, I have an opportunity to practice my preventive medicine teaching and education, which I consider all-important.

Dr. Williams is a gifted physician trained in internal medicine. He is a gifted diagnostician, so he eventually found his place in medicine, just as I have and nurse practitioner Marinetta Van Lahr has. This is all part of the free enterprise system I believe in so strongly. I am convinced that Obamacare, if not repealed, will destroy our wonderful system. You should have the right to choose your own health care provider, and health care providers should have the right to choose where they fit into the system.

What more can I say about Breckinridge County? Good rich agriculture land, good schools, good churches, good recreation, good people, and good neighbors raising good kids. What more can you ask for? I have been blessed! I have always wanted to live up to the faith that Breckinridge County has in me and have done my best to provide them with the best medical care possible.

Throughout my practice I have always used the best specialists I know and would try my best to get my complicated patients to the right specialist, at the right hospital or tertiary care center, at the right time, at the least possible cost to the patient. I have always been aware of the cost of medical care for my patients and tried to keep the cost down. There are many situations where the physician can keep the cost down and not compromise the outcome or fail to meet the standards of good medical care. Often, too many laboratory tests and X-rays are ordered which are not necessary, in my opinion. This is one of the trends in medicine that upsets us "old docs" and has added to the prohibitive cost of medical care.

I think physicians should always keep the cost of the patient's care in mind and help keep the cost down. I don't believe in ordering tests to "cover my backside." I have never practiced medicine looking over my shoulder for the lawyers waiting for me to make a mistake. I have been involved in only two minor lawsuits in my career and none for the past twenty-one years.

When I started my practice fifty-three years ago we were still fee for service, which is the only system that ever made any sense to me. Medicaid and Medicare were gradually phased in early on in my practice and, admittedly, tripled my income, but were the start of misuse and abuse of medical care in America. I have gone through each and every change in medical care for the past fifty-two years including DRGs (hospital payment per case), which is the most stupid system of payment, to Obamacare, which is the worst thing that ever happened to our country. To be sure, before Obama's so-called Affordable Care Act, we had definite problems that needed an answer, including the uninsured, the uninsurable, keeping our insurance when we go from one employer to another or one state to another, having access to insurance outside of our state, setting limits on medical malpractice awards, and others. Tort reform is long past overdue. The outrageous cost of drugs also needs to be addressed.

Obamacare was passed to correct these obvious problems that affected the minority and replaced those problems with an unworkable and unaffordable system that affects 100% of us. It must be repealed!

The last time I looked, the hospital was charging $100 for my office calls. Fifty-two years ago, I started with $3 office calls. Can you imagine that?! I have provided hundreds of thousands of dollars' worth of free medical care to my patients over the past fifty-two years. I have arrived at retirement age without any significant savings but have no regrets.

When Dr. John E. Kincheloe practiced in the early 1900s, he was often paid with chickens, eggs, vegetables, and hay for his horses. Only 50% of the people paid for their medical care. Someone found one of his old ledgers at a yard sale and gave it to me. I passed it on to his grandson, Dale Kincheloe, a fourth-generation Kincheloe physician who is an orthopedic surgeon. He was very excited to get the ledger and very appreciative. It definitely belongs in the Kincheloe family.

When I received the ledger, the first thing I looked for was the P.B. Chambliss account. I was pleased to see that it was paid in full. I also noted that an entry 12-19-1937, my birthday, read "DELIVERY – BABY BOY - $15 PAID." I was elated that I had been one of the 50% who was paid for. For you who do not know, ask a friend how much they paid for a recent delivery! Shocking, isn't it?

Earlier in this book I told you about Dr. John E. Kincheloe Day at the end of his legendary career. He was highly honored and respected. I am sure his last entry in his *LIFE'S LEDGER* was "PAID IN FULL."

Like Dr. John Kincheloe, for the privilege of practicing medicine in Breckinridge County you can put me down for *PAID IN FULL – BACK HOME WHERE I BELONG*.

CHAPTER 14

The Best Office Staff in America

A family physician's practice is only as successful as the quality of his staff! I have often said I have always had the best office staff in America, and most local residents agree. At one time I had two valedictorians and one salutatorian on my staff. Only in a small rural town could this be possible, because in the city they would have been hired by larger organizations or corporations making salaries not available in Hardinsburg. Even so, I paid my staff a premium salary for our community, with the best benefits in town. I consider it to be the best investment I ever made.

I have never been intimidated by someone more intelligent than I, and it has always served me well. I pay them the respect they deserve, and they have been loyal to me through the years.

Patients not only bond to their family physician, but to his staff. Often, the patients don't come to see me as much as to see their friend on the office staff, and their visit is not complete until they have seen and visited with them. Sometimes it is the office nurse, sometimes the office receptionist, sometimes the lab technician, sometimes the office manager, sometimes the insurance clerk, sometimes the transcriptionist. When all is said and done, they spent only 10-15% of their visit with me and 85% of their visit with the staff.

My staff has always acted as a team and bonded together as a family. We laugh together, cry together, and treat each other with love and respect. Laughter frequently permeates the office except, of course, when it is not appropriate during serious encounters. Each employee at one time or another has said they wouldn't work anywhere else. They enjoy their work, which is important.

I've always cross-trained the staff. Everyone knows how to do the other's job so when someone is sick or falls behind, one of the staff will fill in without being asked or told. When they need a day off, they arrange for their own cover, most of the time not needing to consult with me. They know that if the position is covered, it will be alright with me.

Most of the staff let it be known that my office was the place they wanted to work. So, when a position came available, I knew whom to ask. On one occasion I was negotiating salary with one of my previous RNs who was freed up after putting her last child in college and wanting to return to work. She said, "Pay me whatever you want. I just want to work for you." How can you account for an attitude like this? For one thing, we all enjoy taking care of the practice, which we all consider to be family in our small town and treat them as such. We definitely have always tried to create a family atmosphere.

Secondly, I tell each employee, most of whom are raising a family or enjoying grandchildren, that their family comes first. When their kids are sick, or involved in some school or sports activity, they need to be with them. All I ask is that they arrange for a replacement. Would you believe no one has ever abused this? It, in fact, makes them more reliable and happy that they can work without their families feeling neglected.

We celebrate everyone's birthday, and every Christmas season on a work day we close the office for three or four hours and all go to my house for the kind of delightful home-cooked Christmas meal that only my wife can put together, and we exchange gifts. The staff usually combines their resources and gives my wife and me tickets to a University of Kentucky basketball game and reservations at the Hyatt Hotel attached to Rupp Arena. For my birthday their gift is often a U of K basketball print or UK Wildcat paraphernalia. They know how to light me up! But most precious is the Christmas hug I get from each of them with an "I love you, Doctor" or "I appreciate you, Doctor" or "Thanks for everything you do."

I love all my staff, and I think they know I do. They tell their family, friends, and neighbors and always look out for my best interest. They try as hard as I do to build and protect the practice and give the best service possible to our community. They all work very hard without complaining.

It was my good fortune that my office manager, Linda Holloway, came with the practice forty-seven years ago and has been with me every step of the way. Her story is unique and deserves special recognition.

She started working for Cecil Butler in the Soil Conservation office June 1, 1964, three days after graduating co-valedictorian with Bobby Trent in the Breckinridge County High School class of 1964 at the age of sixteen. From 1966 to 1969 she worked for Dr. Carroll James, a local family practice physician. When Dr. James returned to Indiana and turned his practice over to me, Linda agreed to stay with the practice. We would have been lost without her.

She is the best office manager ever and knows more about my business than I do. Not only do I depend on her, the staff and our patients also depend on her and love her. She has dedicated her life to our practice and to her family.

She is a rare combination of high intelligence and common sense. She is reliable, dependable, punctual, fast, and efficient. She runs the office smoothly and commands respect from everyone in the office and community. Everyone takes their problems to Linda, and she has the right answers. She has a great sense of humor, and her humility and pleasant demeanor are contagious.

While working full time and driving from Leitchfield, thirty miles away, every day after her husband established a business there, she raised a beautiful, successful family. Judy, her oldest daughter, has her master's in speech therapy and is employed at Stonecrest Medical Center in Smyrna, Tennessee. Judy's son, Anthony, recently completed his pediatric residency and returned to Grayson County to practice medicine. In February, 2016, Anthony and his wife Jessica made our office manager a great- grandmother by giving birth to a beautiful baby boy. I never dreamed we would have a great-grandmother on the office staff.

Heather, her youngest daughter, is an RN working as a surgical nurse at Twin Lakes Regional Medical Center in Leitchfield and is currently working toward her masters degree in Information Technology. She is married to Steven Smith, a Cecilian Bank executive, and they have two children—Eli, age ten, and Hannah, age seven.

In addition to all this, Linda has been the pianist for the Leitchfield United Methodist Church for many years. Linda will retire soon, and no one ever deserved it more. Speaking on behalf of my office staff, our patients, and the entire Breckinridge County community, we wish her the best. Fifty years (to the day) in one office! An amazing record and an amazing success story for a farm girl from SeRee in Breckinridge County. We all love her dearly!

All my staff deserve equal recognition. They have raised good families and are a special asset to Breckinridge County, and I am proud of them all.

Marinetta Van Lahr, our nurse practitioner, is still working in her nineteenth year, Kathy Brumfield, insurance clerk, in her twenty-second year, and LaDonna Glenn, transcriptionist, in her fourteenth year. After I sold the practice to the local hospital and started working for them in November 2011, Shirley Winchell, our second-longest- working employee as lab and radiology technician, retired after thirty-seven years of service. Fonda Roach, receptionist for thirty-one years; Kristy Pate, receptionist for ten years; and Susan Robinson, RN for eleven years, were forced to find employment with better salaries and health insurance than the hospital offered, to cover their families. Every one of them was the best in their position, and are still loyal, faithful, friends. I will be eternally grateful for their service and was saddened by their departure.

Three employees have died of cancer during their tenure in the office. Don Young, our lab and radiology technician, died at age sixty-one after thirty-one years of service. He also served as Mayor of Hardinsburg. Marilyn Butler, RN, my niece, died at age fifty-five after twenty-five years of service, and Sharon Kennedy, RN, age fifty-six, died after thirteen years of service.

While they were dying, we took care of them like family and tended to their families' needs. Our grief was like losing a best friend or like a parent losing a child. Their smiling faces are still on display at the office in our annual Christmas photos. We talk of them often and remember the good times and remember their dedication in caring for the sick. They are gone but not forgotten. All three were outstanding Christians and are with God today.

Doctors all over America, have sold their practices to their local hospitals. Since then I have seen the "other side of management," and it leaves a lot to be desired; however, it has its good points, and we are adjusting to it. Adjusting to electronic medical records has been stressful for our patients, because it has limited the number of patients we can see and cut our accessibility in half.

Thinking back, I have been blessed and have had the opportunity to practice medicine during the "Golden Age of Medicine."

But despite the entire ever-increasing bureaucratic hassle, there will always be sick people and always be a need for medical care. We will meet their needs. Perhaps with a little less laughter and a little more grumbling, but the love between our patients and their medical care providers will continue. That's what keeps us going!

Janet and staff at annual Christmas feast

Front row: Marinetta Van Lahr, Susan Robinson, Shirley Winchell
Middle row: Linda Roe, Linda Holloway
Back row: LaDonna Glenn, Kathy Brumfiedl, Fonda Roach, Kristy Pate, Jenni West

CHAPTER 15

Best Doctor's Wife in America

My success, more than any other thing, has been because of my wife. I tell her this frequently. We have been total partners since we started to medical school in the fall of 1959 after marrying that summer. I was twenty-one and she was nineteen, about to be twenty in October, though I still tease her about marrying a teenager.

My patients and hospital nurses through the years have told me that my wife is the sweetest and most accommodating doctor's wife they have ever known. When they call looking for me, she is kind and sympathetic and will go to any extreme to get me to the phone, the emergency room, the hospital, the delivery room, or wherever I am needed. She accepts the same degree of urgency that the nurse or patient expresses. The patient knows without question that she is on their side in getting me to address their problem.

Many times after office hours, she has driven to the back of the farm, to a sports event, the lake, or wherever I might be to deliver a message and tell me where I am needed. When we first started in practice, I didn't even have a car phone, much less a smartphone, which is always at my side now. In the meantime, while waiting for me to make my appearance, she loves to give personal advice – always explaining that it is "on the basis of my experience as a mother, or personal experience" claiming no medical training.

She, in fact, has no medical training and strongly believes a doctor's wife should not work in his office, because doctor's wives become too defensive of the abuse and unreasonable expectations all doctors deal with. She also believes all the doctor's employees perform better and are more comfortable when the doctor's wife is not working in the office.

She does believe, however, in befriending all the employees, building them up, bragging on them, talking to them about their kids and sympathizing with their problems. They all love her and light up when she comes to the office to visit. They would do anything for her, and likewise, she would do anything for them.

She loves to talk and to make friends, and knows everybody in town. She makes friends everywhere she goes. Through the years my patients have identified themselves as "I'm your wife's grocery store friend" or "I'm your wife's beauty shop friend" or "I'm your wife's Wal-Mart friend" or "pharmacy friend" or recently, "physical therapy friend" and a never-ending group of "telephone friends." Wherever her activities lead her, she leaves a trail of friends behind.

How does one make so many friends? Obviously – by being a friend. First of all, she has an irrepressible smile and talks to everyone of all ages, male or female, from all social levels and all walks of life on their level. She talks about their interests, their families, and their things, whatever it is. She talks to them about what they are doing and about what she is doing with such enthusiasm that people are attracted to her. She is always willing to do anything for anybody at any time! On the other hand, she will ask them to do things for her which they usually do gladly with equal enthusiasm, much to the shock and surprise of her melancholy husband who would seldom dare ask anyone for anything! I have often been embarrassed by what she asks people to do only to get a reply, "Oh, that's alright. They wanted to." Such is the epitome of a natural-born Sanguine.

She never tires of talking on the phone. She even has a headset so she can fix our meals and do her housework while talking at the same time. I once overheard her having a great visit with someone for twenty-five or thirty minutes. After hanging up I asked her who she was having such a good time talking to. She said, "I don't know – a wrong number. Someone from South Carolina!" Another Sanguine I'm sure!

She will talk to anyone, anytime, anyplace. Everyone knows her voice. When she dials a wrong number in our small town, she will say "I'm sorry" and the other party often says, "That's alright, Janet." She has mastered every word in the vocabulary except the word "good-bye." Every event is presented in length with great detail, chronologically, usually beginning with "The Creation." Life has never been dull at the Chambliss house.

When she talks, I am a very poor listener, and she says I have selective hearing. I admit I do. Sometimes after a long discourse she will say, "Now I really want you to listen to this." I think, and sometimes say to her, "What about the last twenty minutes before that?" She knows I don't listen well. After years of this selective hearing, I have become hard of hearing and now have two hearing aids. My punishment for not listening? Maybe!

My success at being as productive as two ordinary doctors is because of the good care she has taken of me. She has, for years as the boys were growing up, provided three sit down home-cooked meals a day with proper attention to my nutrition. We still do this at noon. If my cardiologist prescribed a low-cholesterol diet, which he did, then she was going to see that I got a low-cholesterol diet.

Years ago, bran muffins were in vogue, so she went overboard (her nature) in preparing bran muffins. I ate them faithfully for a few weeks; then I said one day, "Don't fix any more bran muffins. I would rather have a heart attack."

I do tolerate all of her vitamins, which consist of multiple vitamins, Vitamin D, and large doses of Coenzymes Q-10, which she read was good for my heart and delays dementia. So far they have worked--for the dementia part, anyway.

The first year I practiced medicine, I paid a visit to Dr. C. C. Howard, a noted surgeon in Glasgow, Kentucky, about thirty miles away. It was noon, and he was about eighty-five years old at the time and still practicing surgery. His elderly nurse, a matronly lady near seventy-five herself, told me Dr. Howard was taking his noon nap and she would let me visit him at one o'clock. She was nice, but very protective.

At one o'clock sharp, Dr. Howard came out totally refreshed, alert, and rested. He said, "Bob, I have taken these noon naps all my career, and if you will do this you will extend your career by ten to twenty years." I have followed his advice, and at age seventy-eight I'm still practicing full time and enjoying it. My wife is equally protective and seldom lets anyone disturb me from twelve-thirty to one o'clock unless it's an emergency.

She also takes care of other important needs. Her mother taught her before she married that if a wife would take care of all of her husband's needs, she would never have to worry about him straying. I have thanked my wise mother-in-law for this advice a thousand times in my own mind.

I had the best mother-in-law in the world and often told her she was. I expressed to my wife several times that when she got older I wanted her to be just like her mother. As always, wives do things that irritate their husbands. When I show my irritation, my wife says to me, "Now my mother did that or was like that when she got older and you said you wanted me to be just like my mother." You can't win them all! But I have learned that if you brag on your wife a lot and say "thank you" a lot, and "I appreciate you" a lot, and "I love you" a lot, it goes a long way.

How do I best describe my wife? I once attended a motivational seminar and we were asked by the speaker to write down ten things that would describe our mate. I wrote the following, not necessarily in this order, and, as you can see, I didn't limit it to ten. For obvious reasons, I started the list with "enthusiastic." Here is my complete list:

- Enthusiastic •
- Kind and considerate •
- Devoted wife and "Mother of the Year" type •
- Sincere Christian •
- Excellent teacher •
- Outstanding lover •
- Fantastic cook •
- Hard worker •
- Giving and caring person •
- Classy and pretty •
- Honest and open •
- Loyal and dependable •
- Sensitive with an uncanny intuition •
- Friendly and likable •
- Prone to overdo things •
- Black belt shopper •
- Marathon talker*

I think Janet will best be remembered as an eternal cheerleader. She was a cheerleader in high school, a cheerleader in college, a cheerleader for our three boys, and, I'm sure, for our future grandchildren. When she goes to Heaven, I'm quite sure she will be a cheerleader. I can see her now leading the applause for the saints and praise rallies for her God. "Come on, you all! Let's hear it for Jehovah!"

I met her in high school. I played basketball for Breckinridge County High School, and she led cheers for the Hancock County High School, our rival. I wasn't especially attracted to cheerleaders. However, I couldn't help but notice this one cheerleader from Hancock County. I liked the way she was friendly with everyone and always had an infectious smile exposing her beautiful white teeth. I liked the way she filled out her sweater. I liked the way she watched the ballgame and cheered her players on, unlike the others who primped and paraded up the sidelines, at times more aware of the cheering section than the game. "Defense" she would yell. "Watch that pick!" "Five seconds are up!" "Watch the back door!" "Four fouls, Billy!" "That's alright. You can do it!"

This gal knew her basketball. She also knew how to win and how to lose. When they won, she didn't gloat. When they lost, she didn't cry. She once told me, "I never understood the other cheerleaders crying over a loss. What I did," she said, "was go have a good time after the game. But that night I would play the game over and over in my mind." I was impressed, because that's what I did.

She also knew the opposition. "Good game, Bobby!" She knew my name! She told me, "I would always tell our players, you better stop that Chambliss boy from Breckinridge County." Wow! This gal knew talent when she saw it!

I used to see her in the summer at Indian Lake where we went swimming. I liked the way she was friendly with everyone, and she was always smiling. I liked the way she swam – gliding through the water quietly like a graceful swan, with hardly a ripple.

She went to Campbellsville College, a small Baptist Junior College, where she was a cheerleader. I went to the University of Kentucky. In the summer of 1958, I was at Indian Lake again, lying on a wooden float suspended by barrels in the middle of the lake recuperating from my sophomore year when "the cheerleader" came gliding up to the float. "Hi, Bobby. How was your school year?" We talked for a long time. Conversation came easy to the cheerleader.

I had never dated her; in fact, I had never dated anyone seriously. Dating was expensive, and I was hoarding my money for college. As she started to leave, I asked her if she was doing anything that night; if not, maybe we could get together. She said, "It's Sunday night and I always go to church, but you can come with me."

I thought, *There's no way I'm going to go to church on a first date.* "You can't miss this one time?" I asked.

"No!" she said firmly. "How about Saturday night?"

"Great!"

I was to learn that there were some things the cheerleader would never compromise. I was impressed. Our mutual stubbornness that started there that day at Indian Lake was sure to rear its head again over and over in years to come.

A hot summer romance followed this early June encounter. We were together as many times as I could get off from work, and sometimes I would miss work – a rarity for me, as you can surmise.

I had always had in mind the kind of gal I wanted to be the mother of my children, but in the summer of 1958, looking for that special person was the farthest thing from my mind. I had two more years of pre-med, four years of medical school, and very little money, so I had plans to start looking after medical school.

One night toward the end of a full and romantic summer, while driving home late at night on Indian Lake Hill, it suddenly occurred to me that she was the one I wanted to spend the rest of my life with. It shocked me that it even entered my mind, but once the thought was in place, I could think of nothing else. I wondered how I would feel and how she would feel when we went back to our respective colleges and busy schedules.

I kept the thought private but gave her my fraternity pin and a bracelet made up of all my honor "keys" I had earned being a B.M.O.C. at the University of Kentucky. I had worked hard at all the extra-curricular activities, which eventually resulted in my being named the Outstanding Fraternity Man on Campus during Greek Week my junior year, and I was the heir apparent for the student body president the following year. But my interest in campus affairs was never the same again after a summer with the cheerleader, and after school started in the fall, I kept returning to Campbellsville College to see her.

I was recommended by the Dean of the Arts and Science College for early admission to the Vanderbilt University School of Medicine after my third year of pre- med, so I dropped my pursuit of the student body presidency and started a personal campaign for her hand and approval of her parents to marry their daughter and take her out of school at Campbellsville and take her with me to medical school at Vanderbilt in Nashville, Tennessee. I won both campaigns which was greater than any of my achievements at the University of Kentucky, by far.

Her mother was somewhat reluctant, but finally said to Janet, "Yes, you have my blessings. I can tell by the way Bob looks at you – it's time to marry." Such a wise lady! I was madly in love and didn't want to go to medical school without her. Her mother had wanted so badly for Janet to be a teacher and the first college graduate in the family. I spent the rest of my mother-in-law's life (she lived to ninety) being exceptionally good to her and trying to make it up to her. No one could love their mother-in-law more. I might add, it was not hard to do.

We had no money. I had to borrow money from my dad to get her a ring. I told my father I had found a gal just like the one he married, and he gave me the money quickly with an approving smile. He loved her, too, and they had a wonderful relationship until his death at age eighty-four.

In the early fall of 1957 after our summer together, I drove to Campbellsville, proposed to her, and she enthusiastically accepted. She did everything with enthusiasm.

I have always treated her with love and respect. I wish I could say I have never hurt her feelings, but I cannot. Many times I have made her cry, and I wished to God I had not. Two strong-willed, outspoken people cannot live under the same roof without hurting each other. But I never hurt her that I didn't feel just as bad or worse, and, thank God, she has never failed to forgive me, and I have never failed to forgive her – the secret of a long marriage, because there is no relationship without hurt requiring forgiveness.

Enthusiasm, I have discovered, is the key to all success. The word enthusiasm means "God within" and it is our enthusiasm that shows the world that God lives within us – in our hearts. Children and dogs always know if our heart is right. Some people do, too. She has taught seven-year-olds in Sunday School for thirty years. It is amazing what she can do with seven-year-olds. You can go by her class, and she always has ten or fifteen children spellbound, in the palm of her hand, like the Pied Piper. She plays games with them, tells them stories, makes flannel board presentations, and has creative activities. She is always motivational with a desired end result. They love her and cry when they are promoted on to the next level and never forget her. They cry, and she cries. During the two years she has them "in her care," she thoughtfully and carefully presents them with God's love and plan of salvation. She becomes intimate and involved in their family life, problems, and lifestyle and usually keeps up with them for the rest of their lives. She now has former students bringing their children in for her instruction and guidance, and I wouldn't be surprised if the third generation doesn't show up soon. I know that God must smile on this one servant's activities – or as our church members say, "Janet doing her thing with the kids." She taught the children how to love God, love others, and love themselves.

She would hug them every Sunday morning when they came in and taught them that hugging is important. Twenty to thirty years later, big ol' boys and men still come up to her in Wal-Mart or wherever and give her a big hug. They love her dearly, and she has been a great influence on a lot of lives in Breckinridge County.

Sometimes her enthusiasm has gotten out of control. One year she was chairman of the county fair parade. She promoted it so enthusiastically that it was the longest parade in the history of the county. The parade was so long, in fact, the traffic was backed up for miles and no one could get through Hardinsburg for two hours. This was before we had a bypass. They never asked her to be a parade chairman again! But we've never had a parade again that would come close to equaling that one.

She can even get involved with the TV. You hear a lot now about interactive TV. Her viewing has always been interactive! She warns TV characters of impending danger shouting, "Look out!" or "Don't believe that!" She can be heard cheering them on, or if it's sad, there will be tears streaming down her cheeks. There is no shame or holding back with her emotions. What you see is what you get! You never have to wonder where you stand.

She is the epitome of the "old-fashioned" values of honesty, loyalty, dependability and fairness – sometimes carrying them to great extremes, often unreasonable extremes or sometimes, in the minds of her family, inconvenient extremes. She would rather die than tell you a lie or tell you she will do something and not do it.

An example of these extremes are lists she keeps at Christmas of all her purchases for our three boys, making sure that she spends the same on all three to the exact penny. The boys have never doubted that they have been treated "fair." This same sense of fairness dictates her actions in all her relationships, which is good, but it distresses her when she is not treated fairly. She is distressed with social unfairness and social injustice which, of course, dominate our modern society.

She is intensely loyal and dependable. You can count on her to do her part and to be there when you need her. You may invoke her ire or judgement for outrageous behavior – but she will forgive and stay with you until the bitter end.

She likes nice things but was always satisfied when we had nothing. Money means nothing to her, but relationships are everything. Through the years I noticed that if I came home and said I made a thousand dollars today, she would say "Great!" or if I said I made three thousand dollars today, she would say "Great!" – the same "Great!" for very unequal results. It doesn't mean a thing to her. What means something is that I'm "busting my behind" for her and our boys.

Big things have never impressed her – a Cadillac – a large diamond ring – a big house, etc. She enjoys them very much, but it doesn't get nearly the response as remembering her special days, helping clear the table, doing her chores when she is tied up with other activities, taking her out to eat when she is tired, understanding when she has a "little problem" on her mind, listening when she needs to talk out a problem, or complimenting her on a job well done, or, as our boys say, "Doing one of her momma things," or simply cuddling up and watching a home movie or any little courtesy or kindness. The song "Little Things Mean a Lot" could have been written about her.

She has devoted most of her life to our three boys. I have often said that her enthusiasm has been indelibly stamped on our three sons' personalities, and a lot of their past and future success can be attributed to this.

We were fortunate that Janet could be a stay-at-home mom. Her life was dedicated to raising three boys, quite an experience for a gal who had no brothers. At this she excelled and raised three fine sons who are very accomplished. We did this together with much fun and satisfaction.

She took care of my parents who lived next door and lived until age eighty-four and eighty-eight. They loved her with a passion, and my mother told me many times if I left her to not bother about coming home. She said, "I don't want to hear another story of a woman working to put her husband through medical school who later leaves her for another woman." I was forewarned!

I learned a lot from Janet through the years. I have learned that sharing is more important than accumulating. Presence is more important than presents. I have learned that caring is more important than being correct; being together is more important than a tidy house; companionship is more important than winning; and loving is more important than providing. In fact, the bottom line is that loving is more important than anything.

Our anniversaries have reached fifty-seven at this time, and nothing has changed except for a few more irritations of her overprotecting me, and giving me more advice than I want to hear on how I should take care of myself. She makes up for that by praying for me daily. I'm trying my best not to be a "grumpy old man." We take turns trying to decide who will die first, and I'm quite sure it will be me. Her mother was ninety.

I can rest assured, should I predecease her, that her telephone skills will keep her going and she will have hundreds of people who will provide for her every need, including her three sons. She has given her whole life to me, her family, her church, and her community.

Is "the cheerleader" a perfect mom and a perfect wife? No! No more than I'm perfect or you are perfect, but it's hard to fault someone who respects you more than you deserve, who promotes you more than you deserve, and who loves you more than you deserve. She is my eternal cheerleader. I'm going to hold on to her – hopefully, for an eternity.

Sue Bruner
"Best mother-in-law in America"

Grammy and grandsons, Cooper and Caleb

Janet's parents, Francis and Sue Bruner
Hawesville, KY

CHAPTER 16

Tribute to My Colleagues

Just as it is vitally important to have a good working relationship with your office staff, it is important to have a good working relationship with your fellow physicians and health care providers. I have tried through the years to make friends with the best specialists in the closest cities--that is, Louisville, Owensboro, and Elizabethtown--and utilize their talents for my patients.

Early on in my practice, specialists appreciated referrals and would tell you they did. They, in turn, would comment favorably on the treatment and skills of the family physician who referred them patients. So everyone was rewarded; the specialist, the referring family physician, and, most importantly, the patients who needed to be reassured that they were getting the best care possible. This has gradually changed over the years. I miss getting a call or letter from the consultants like we used to. I made friends and built relationships with referring physicians. Now I get a 5-10 page electronic medical record which is usually very confusing, or often I have to call for a report.

It is even more important to develop a close working relationship with your fellow medical providers in the town or county where you practice. When I returned to Hardinsburg, Dr. James Sills, who is also a local product, had returned to Hardinsburg five years earlier and was already well established. He was also a physician who was willing to work day and night. For the next thirty-plus years we almost single-handedly kept the local emergency room going 24/7 in addition to delivering approximately three hundred babies annually and keeping an individual census of ten to fifteen patients each in the local hospital.

As I said earlier, we also went to surgery with all of our patients requiring surgery. If it was my patient, I would be the first assistant to the surgeon, and he would give anesthesia. If it was his patient, he would be the surgical assistant, and I would give the anesthesia. He saw my patients on my day off and weekend off and I, in turn, would see his patients on his day off and weekend off. Over a period of time, we knew each other's patients "inside and out."

There is one patient in town who often reminds me that she went to Dr. Sills four times for her prenatal care, and when it came time for the delivery he was out of town. I delivered all four of her children. He returned the favors – always at no charge.

Dr. Sills never said anything he didn't mean. He recently put this comment on Facebook under my picture that one of my sons had posted on my seventy-eighth birthday: "A great picture of the man who helped me be the family doctor I wanted to be. He was and is a wonderful associate." Dr. Jim Sills, this is one of the most heartwarming compliments I have ever received, and I appreciate it.

Dr. Sills and I are from the old school. We wore suits and ties every day. The younger doctors now wear jeans or scrub suits around the office and hospital, which I will never get used to. They also expect a forty-hour week with full coverage the rest of the time. They complain of being busy seeing thirty patients a day, which I never understood until I sold my practice to the hospital in 2011 and started a similar practice. I know now that thirty patients a day does keep one doctor busy all day from 8:00 – 4:00 with all the paperwork and EMR that's been added to what we are required to do. In my opinion, electronic medical records have made things worse, not better.

The young physicians are all very smart, just as I felt I was in 1964. I had an answer for everything. After I got the confidence and common sense to say, "I don't know" at times, it was more comfortable for both the patient and me. I have a lot of respect for the younger doctors and, admit it or not, we keep an eye on each other's treatment and practice of medicine and learn a lot from each other. That's the way it is supposed to be.

"Old docs" know a lot more than I used to think they know, and younger docs still come out of school confident that they have an answer for every patient's problem. I thank God I have been given the opportunity to see that through the eyes of a twenty-six- year-old and through the eyes of a seventy-nine-year old. It's been fun and rewarding, and I wouldn't trade my legacy for anyone's.

I would be remiss if I did not mention that for many of these years we had an excellent surgeon in the person of Earl Buchele from Centralia, Illinois, who did his residency at the Cook County Hospital in Chicago. Prior to becoming a surgeon, he was a Methodist minister and was the "ultimate happy warrior." He was well trained in general surgery as well as orthopedic surgery and could do an unbelievable variety of procedures. He also worked day and night and was always ready to do our C-sections, appendectomies, or trauma any time we asked.

Often, when he was operating, he would start singing, much to our amusement. He had a unique cackle I would recognize a hundred years from now if I heard it again. Unfortunately, he died a premature death at the age of forty-nine with lymphoma – tragic for him and his family (wife and four brilliant sons) and tragic for

Breckinridge County. I think of him more often than any other professional who has preceded me and always smile when he comes to mind.

Breckinridge County has always had outstanding nurses. They are the center of good medical care and akin to angels. They have my respect and love. I have often said that nurses are the most important people in the delivery of medical care. They are usually the patient's first contact. They do all the hard, unpleasant work, and when people die, they are often holding a nurse's hand--and most of the time, there is a tear in the nurse's eye.

They work nights, weekends, holidays, and they work when they don't feel like it. Most of them love their work and love their patients and listen to all their complaints and fears. They give good advice – always teaching. I have had the privilege of being associated with some of the finest nurses ever. I appreciate their hard work and dedication and I tell them often that I do. I appreciate their opinions and common sense and often it is the nurse who makes the right diagnosis and helps with the physician's decision making.

It is a wise physician who recognizes their skills and importance in taking care of patients and works together with them in providing medical care. I respect them and let them know that I do.

I have served on several boards through the years including the Breckinridge County Board of Education, serving as chairman, Board of Health, Board of Trustees Farmers Bank of Hardinsburg, and the Breckinridge Memorial Hospital Board of Directors to name a few, but none as outstanding as the Breckinridge Memorial Hospital Board of Directors. Through the years it has been made up of the most gifted and dedicated members of our county who have dedicated themselves to providing outstanding hospital care and medical services to Breckinridge County.

In my forty-seven years of affiliation with the Breckinridge Memorial Hospital, the board has been operated 100% free of any political interference from county officials who lease the property to Breckinridge Health Inc. They have built new and improved facilities and added diagnostic facilities and procedures we never dreamed possible for a rural hospital, including MRI, MRA, CAT scans, CTA of the chest, digital mammography, most ultrasound procedures including echocardiogram, nuclear medicine including bone scans, myocardial profusion studies, gastric emptying, HIDA scans, lung VQ, renograms, thyroid uptakes and scans and many others including most lab studies.

Our board members are forward-looking and learn everything they can about hospital administration, national and state health care policies, and local needs. They are always looking to the future and always make the best decisions possible for our county hospital.

Despite federal and state bureaucracy, they have kept our hospital solvent and "state of the art" for a small rural hospital. I have enjoyed a good working relationship with them and had the privilege to serve with them as the representative from the hospital staff for many years.

The local nursing home is located next to my office. I have always complimented them for having the best-operated and cleanest nursing home in Central Kentucky. I have served as their medical director for many years and have enjoyed the affiliation.

Fortunately, the hospital emergency room is directly across the street which is most convenient, giving our nursing home patients quick access to the local hospital, emergency room, pharmacy, and physician.

We have three home-owned pharmacies operated by second- and third-generation hometown pharmacists who are all extremely competent. They participate in the total delivery of health care by teaching and monitoring and providing home deliveries and surgical supplies.

Breckinridge County operates a well-organized health department and several home health agencies that serve the county well. Dr. Sills came out of retirement for several years and provided house calls for our elderly homebound patients – a service appreciated by all the local physicians and the elderly and their families.

Medical care is definitely a team effort, and I have been appreciative of everyone who does his/her part. Cooperation has always been a collective effort.

Dr. Jim Sills and Dr. Chambliss making rounds at the local hospital.

CHAPTER 17

Family Comes First: Building Three Sons

Build Me A Son
by General Douglas MacArthur

> *Build me a son,*
> *O Lord, who will be strong enough to know when he*
> *is weak, and brave enough to face himself when he is*
> *afraid; one who will be proud and unbending in honest*
> *defeat, and humble and gentle in victory.*
> *Build me a son whose wishes will not take the place of deeds;*
> *a son who will know Thee – and that to know himself is the*
> *foundation stone of knowledge.*
> *Lead him, I pray, not in the path of ease and comfort, but*
> *under the stress and spur of difficulties and challenge. Here let*
> *him learn to stand up in the storm; here let him learn compassion*
> *for those who fail.*

Build me a son whose heart will be clear, whose goal will be high,
a son who will master himself before he seeks to master other
men, one who will reach into the future,
yet never forget the past.
And after all these things are his,
add, I pray, enough of a sense of
humor, so that he may always be serious,
yet never take himself too seriously.
Give him humility, so that he may
always remember the simplicity of true
greatness, the open mind of true wisdom,
and the meekness of true strength.
Then, I, his father, will dare to
whisper, "I have not lived in vain."

I hit the ground running when I got home and never looked back. I worked at least 14-15 hours a day 24/7 which, of course, took most of my available time and often took away from my sleeping time, since most babies seem to be born at night.

I was happy doing this, but had made a promise to myself that I would spend enough time with my three sons to help mold them into the men described so insightfully by General McArthur, famous World War II and Korean War general.

I have heard my colleagues justify the time they spend with their children by saying that they spend quality time with them. It is my opinion that much more is needed than quality time--it takes lots of time every day. You develop a better relationship with your sons down on the floor wrestling with them, playing ball with them, working with them, going to the creek or lake, and never missing a ballgame or any school event they are involved with.

How do you do this working 14-15 hours a day? *You plan to do it, and then you do it.* I never wasted a minute! Fortunately, our family farm is next to the hospital and our home is on top of a hill near the hospital. Nurses at the hospital at one time could look out the second-floor window of the hospital and observe me come and go. One day a nurse called my wife and asked to speak to me.

My wife said, "Dr. Chambliss isn't here. He's at the hospital."

The nurse answered "No, I see him going into the garage right now."

Not only is my house close by; my office is directly across the road behind the hospital and is located between our local nursing home and pharmacy. The hospital was built on property owned by my grandmother at one time. My office was built on the Chambliss farm owned by my uncle.

When I returned home, I told my Uncle Vernon I was coming home to practice medicine and would like to buy an acre or two on which to build a medical office. He said, "I won't sell it to you," then after a pause, with a smile said, "but I will give it to you." He became my patient and eventually died in the hospital across the street directly in front of his house.

So why am I telling you all this? Because of the close proximity to my work, I had no wasted time in the car and devoted all the spare time I could to the boys for work and play (both important). That small amount of time, however, was minuscule compared to the time their mother had with them. She devoted her entire life to the boys, and I called her the "best boy's mother" in the world.

We had three home-cooked sit-down meals every day, after they were properly blessed. Mealtime gave us the opportunity to catch up on everyone's activities of the day. Laughter was always present, and mischievous teasing most of the time. At times there were four to six boys or more around the table. Occasionally they would throw a biscuit rather than pass it, but for the most part we taught them good manners, and they were good conversationalists and debaters. They still say "Yes, sir," "No, sir," "Please," "Thank you," etc. Like most boys, the funniest thing is usually something gross; the more gross and disgusting, the better! Their mother got a full education, raising boys. They showed their love and appreciation by playfully teasing her.

One of the funniest things to happen occurred one day when I was playing baseball with the boys in the large yard between our house and my parents' house. We had our infield bases in place. My parents' house was in center field. I was up to bat and Jim threw me a perfect pitch. I swung hard and hit a line drive right into the side of Mom and Dad's house, knocking a large hole into the side of the house, which was covered with brittle siding.

I had never hit a ball that far. I immediately said, "I had better go apologize to Mom and Dad and reassure them that I will have it repaired." We always taught the boys to respect others' property. As I walked sheepishly across the yard I could see the boys rolling on the lawn laughing hysterically over the sight of seeing their father have to apologize to his parents for knocking a hole in their house. This always comes up with laughter at Christmas dinners and reminiscing times. It was one of those good "teaching moments" you can have only when you are with your children.

Like their father, all three of our boys were involved in extracurricular activities: sports, agriculture projects, school projects, public speaking, and church activities. For years, their mother was the family chauffeur from one location to another, to another. I was happy when Bryan reached age sixteen and could help with the transportation. By sixteen, farm boys are experienced drivers, so we didn't worry until we got to Jim, our second son.

Our worry was well grounded with Jim. He had an accident the first day he got his driver's license. Jim was a child who was born with no fear. He eventually survived his childhood only to do such things as bungee jump off the world's highest suspension bridge in New Zealand, sky dive from planes, and ski on the double black diamond slopes of Colorado. While practicing law in Vail, Colorado, he was a ski instructor and spent weekends conducting white water rafting tours down the Colorado River (class C and D rafting). Likewise, he has little or no fear when he presents his research or Ph.D. thesis at universities all over the world, including the International Epilepsy Congress in Rome, Italy in 2011.

Jim was a hard kid to raise. We often would be shopping in a large department store and look around, and Jim would be gone. In a huge crowd like at Disney World or New York City, he would disappear. Fortunately, we always found him and raised him to college age with a lot of luck and the help of God and "guardian angels."

I tried to teach all three boys by example, as my father had done for me. You may wonder what all this has to do with being a good family physician. A small-town doctor is more than just a person who treats sick people. He is one of the most visible people in the county and has the opportunity to be an example for all and a witness for his faith. Also, a family physician who is happy with his wife, happy with his family, interested and involved in his community, is a well-adjusted physician happy with his life. This makes him more relatable and a better all-around physician who understands and interacts with all his patients.

There is more to life for a doctor than being a doctor. In fact, let me restate that *it's more important to be a parent than a doctor.* My primary goal was always to raise a good family with happy, well-adjusted, ambitious children who in turn would be prepared to make a contribution to their generation.

So even though I did the work of two physicians, I made sure I spent a lot of time with the boys. It has paid great dividends. First of all, we wanted each of them to feel special and unique. We took them to church and taught them the Bible, and each of them at the age of accountability accepted Jesus Christ as his personal Lord and Savior.

We tried to teach them a good work ethic. This wasn't easy! Jim, who was always open and honest, said to me as a ten-year- old,

"Daddy, why do you make me work so hard? You know I don't like to work! We work more than all our friends."

I replied "I am doing it purposely and someday you will thank me for it." We worked hard on the family farm and spent a lot of time in the show barn with the show cattle. Each of the boys had his own show calves and was successful in showing them all over the state. Bryan accepted the challenge and performed well. Jim hated it and when asked why, he replied, "Cows smell bad." He wanted to play football all the time and eventually was allowed to pursue this channel for his abundant energy.

Brad, four years younger, was always competitive and always tried to outdo his older brothers. He grew up in the show barn and eventually showed championship cattle all over the United States.

Bryan, the oldest son, was valedictorian of his high school class and Phi Beta Kappa and Omicron Delta Kappa at Baylor University, Waco, Texas. Academics came easily for Bryan, but he wanted very much to be an athlete, especially a basketball player like his father. He had the height, but unfortunately he was very slender and as he often said, "looked more like a geek" with his thick black-rimmed glasses. But basketball was a hopeless situation for Bryan. Nobody ever tried harder, and the harder he tried and practiced, the more he rode the bench and the more he became discouraged. He was so upset that he couldn't master the round ball that I sat down one night and wrote out a creed that I thought would help him deal with the situation. Eventually he gave up playing basketball, but still "bleeds blue" and still follows University of Kentucky basketball intensely.

"Bryan's Creed" is just another way for a father to give his son advice and help him find his way (like General MacArthur's poem "Building a Son").

BRYAN'S CREED

I will try to remember at all times that basketball is only a game. Being a game, this implies that it is fun or should be fun.

I will be intensely competitive and will do everything within my power to beat you; but after the game is over, we will be friends.

I will try at all times to maintain a good attitude even though I spend most of the time sitting on the bench.

I will try to be enthusiastic and encourage my teammates both off and on the floor.

I will try at all times to remember that there are other members of the team who have less playing time than I do and that they, too, have feelings, hopes, aspirations, and disappointments.

I will not blame the officials, my coach, or my teammates for my own deficiencies.

I will always try to improve myself and, if my talents prove to be less than my teammates, I will accept this.

I will always try to remember that the purpose of basketball and athletics is to teach competitiveness, teamwork, discipline, good sportsmanship, and to promote physical fitness, good health, good fellowship, and a darn good time.

But he was determined to be an athlete and was not going to be denied. He discovered by accident that he could run and jump hurdles, so he began to train harder than any kid in high school, building up his legs and speed. Eventually this 6' 4," 155- pound "geek" shocked all the football players by beating them in sprints and bench pressing.

Breckinridge County High School had no experienced track coach, so Bryan got a book on the techniques of high hurdles and practiced relentlessly, experiencing many painful falls and injuries until he mastered the hurdles. Every race was run with pain, especially the last.

As I implied, Bryan was not athletic, but he had a will to win. More than that, he had the will to prepare to win. He ended up being MVP in track three consecutive years at Breckinridge County High School and as a senior won the conference setting a new mark of 16.3 and finishing fifth in Semi-state. (See sports write-up in the photos at the end of the chapter.) I think this was a remarkable accomplishment for a "geek" who always led his class academically from Breckinridge County Elementary School to Breckinridge County High School to Baylor University to Vanderbilt Medical School to Harvard for his residency training in psychiatry.

At Baylor University he majored in pre-med and English literature and was recipient of several writing awards, including the Baylor University Department of English, E. Hudson Long Award for Creative Writing. (A sample of his writing is included in Appendix B at the back of this book.) During his tenure at Baylor, he was a Cultural Exchange Student at the Seinan Gakuin University in Fukuoka, Japan for one year. While he was there, we got to visit him and rode the "bullet train" all over Japan from city to city and got to visit many historical sites, temples, castles, and places of interest. We had a great time.

The summer after graduation, he married the graduating valedictorian at Baylor Class of 1987, and they have three very outstanding and intelligent daughters, one of whom recently became a National Merit Scholarship finalist.

Bryan attended Vanderbilt Medical School, receiving his MD degree, after which he was accepted into the Harvard Psychiatry Residency Program in Cambridge, Massachusetts. He had additional training at the Harvard University Austin Riggs Center, in Strockbridge, Massachusetts, completing an Advanced Psychiatry Fellowship in Psychodynamic Psychotherapy.

He has served as Director of Residency Training, St. Francis Medical Center, Pittsburgh, and later Director of Psychotherapy

Training, University of Pittsburgh School of Medicine in Pittsburgh. Later he was named Director of Residency Training at the Drexel University College of Medicine in Philadelphia, where he was an Associate Professor of Psychiatry.

He was named Teacher of the Year in 1999, 2001, 2002, 2006, 2008, and 2009 and Faculty Member of the Year in 2005 at Drexel University Medical School. He is now a staff psychiatrist and medical director at the Creative Health Services, Pottstown, Pennsylvania, doing what he loves to do best, practicing clinical psychiatry and using his skills in psychotherapy.

He has authored two chapters in the *Kaplan & Sacock's Comprehensive Textbook of Psychiatry, Ninth Edition,* an internationally used textbook in medical schools around the world. I asked him for his CV (curriculum vitae) and it is thirty pages long! I won't attempt to list all of his awards and accomplishments in his field.

Number two son, Jim, after he got football out of his system, settled down and made mostly A's in college. I told him if he would make a 4.0 GPA (straight A's) his freshman year, I would buy him the new car he had been asking for. That was the one and only time I offered any of the three boys any award for performance, because I don't believe in it. Jim, prone to play and have fun, was deliberately unlike his one-year-older brother, and I thought it was the safest deal I had ever made. Jim collected on it and from that point on was academically oriented, even to the point of winning an academic scholarship to Transylvania University in Lexington. Let me add, this more than paid for his car.

He graduated from the Denver Colorado School of Law and practiced law in Kentucky and near Vail, Colorado for ten years. He is an accomplished skier, which is what attracted him to the Vail area. He also spent his weekends conducting white water rafting trips down the Colorado River, which he loved, and it brought in extra income. He told me one weekend he had the entire officer team of the

American Bar Association in his raft. I asked him what he talked to them about. He replied laughingly, "I told them lawyer jokes. They really got a kick out of them."

One day he was talking to a client's father in a parking lot, and an SUV backed out of a parking space and blindsided him, striking him in the left temple. The results of this unfortunate accident is explained by Byron Crawford, feature writer for the "Louisville Courier Journal". This feature article is included at the end of this chapter. This led Jim to a Masters Degree in art from the University of Louisville and a PhD from the University of Melbourne in art and medicine and research in "how epilepsy affects artistic creativity."

His research continued to gain international attention and he has presented his findings to neurology forums and medical schools all over the world. He co-edited a book entitled *Epilepsy, Perception, Imagination, and Change* when he was getting his PhD from Melbourne University in Australia. He contributed a major chapter to this book concerning his thesis. He is currently writing another book.

His epilepsy is under excellent control on medication, and his cognitive skills, including reading, have returned to normal. He married an Australian and has two beautiful bright children, Zac and Chloe. We are watching them grow up on Skype and have visited Australia three times. We are extremely proud that Jim took something devastating and recovered with great success, a great example of "turning lemons into lemonade." I would like to think that his early home training contributed to his determination to succeed in the face of adversity. If I had one word to describe Jim, it would be "resilient."

Recently he has had other health issues not related to his brain injury but is working his way through them. He is an excellent parent and is dearly loved by his children. He is still excited about his new career and is highly motivated to help others with similar problems.

Number three son, Brad, four years younger than Jim and five younger than Bryan, got off to a slow start academically. When he finished the first grade, we were aware that he couldn't read. We had him examined by a child psychologist, Dr. Lee Epstein, in Louisville, who is a specialist in learning disabilities. Dr. Epstein had worked with some of my more complicated cases, and he diagnosed a reading disability and prescribed a Distar Remedial Reading Program for Brad. We have a special friend, Suellen Raley Whitworth, an elementary teacher, who has some expertise in this area, and she tutored him one-on-one for five or six months.

Brad was sensitive and embarrassed that he couldn't read like the other kids in the second grade and he was teased for being in the "dumb group." So, being a very aggressive and competitive child, he worked on it as hard as he could. This remedial program and tutoring were exactly what he needed, and within a few months he caught up with the other kids and soon passed them in reading ability. He and his parents will be eternally grateful to Suellen and Dr. Epstein. This started within him an attitude of hard work and determination to be the best that he could be. This attitude has stayed with him all his life.

His aggressiveness, competitive attitude, dedication, and winsome personality eventually opened many doors. In time he became National President of the Junior Hereford Association, National Vice President of the Future Farmers of America, at that time a 500,000-member group of high school agricultural students, which provided him opportunities for travel all over the world including Europe, China, and the Far East. He had the privilege as an eighteen-year-old to meet with President Ronald Reagan at the White House and the following year made a formal presentation to President George Bush at the White House.

At the 1989 National Convention of the National FFA Organization in Kansas City, Missouri, attended by 60,000, during the closing session they always have a recognition ceremony for the parents of the retiring national officers. When we were on the platform flanked on one side by the National Chorus and on the other side by the National Band, a little girl from the chorus with a fantastically beautiful voice and expressive eyes sang to us parents the beautiful song "The Wind Beneath My Wings." It was very emotional, and through the tears I could only think of my own parents. What an honor and what a feeling it is to be considered a hero by your children! I am thankful to God that I let my parents know they were my heroes. I really appreciated the tribute to my wife and me.

Brad chose his father's alma mater, which made me very proud, and he got off to a good start by being named Freshman of the Year his first year at the University of Kentucky. He developed into a skilled public speaker, winning several national speaking contests and eventually was the first student at the University of Kentucky to be asked to give a commencement address, along with a noted public figure. The year he graduated, 1992, the Honorable Thomas M. T. Niles, United States Assistant Secretary of State, gave the commencement address and received a modest applause. Brad followed him, and when he finished, received a standing ovation from the 10,000-plus students and their families in the Memorial Coliseum in Lexington.

His CV (curriculum vitae) lists three pages of awards and college achievements which I won't include, but I think reading his challenging commencement address would be worth your time. It is included in Appendix B.

He now has a very successful mortgage company in Elizabethtown, Kentucky and has served as state president of his professional association. He has also continued with the family farming operation and has developed a registered Hereford cattle operation nationally known for its excellence.

He has four sons ages 6-17 and is active with them in multiple sports, and he coaches Little League basketball. His sons are all excellent students and are being brought up like he was, active in sports and church activities. One of them, Clint Robert Chambliss, has already announced his interest in becoming a physician, which will make the third generation of Chambliss physicians. I promote the University of Kentucky with all the grandsons. Caleb, age seven, who enjoys teasing me, says he is going to the University of Wal-Mart.

It has taken all of our income educating and following our children around the world, sharing and enjoying their success. That's what makes life worthwhile. We didn't have anything when we started out on our life's journey, and our eternity has already been taken care of. God is good and has blessed us greatly with nine precious grandchildren and precious memories. Perhaps, in the words of General McArthur, "We have not lived in vain."

Bryan Chambliss Sets Conference Record
Finishes 5th In Semi-State Competition

Bryan Chambliss equaled his time of 16.2 in the semi-state at Richmond Saturday, May 16, and finished 5th in the meet held there. Chambliss had won the regional at North Bullitt the week before with the same time. Early in the track season in a conference meet at Grayson County, Chambliss set a new conference mark of 16.3. The old record for the conference was 17.2 and that also belonged to Chambliss.

In the meet at Richmond Saturday the winner of the 120 yard high hurdles was Jack Smalley of Boyle County. Ironically, in the semi-state last year, Bryan beat Smalley. The fifth place finish at this level caps off Chambliss' career as a track man at Breckinridge County.

Bryan ran cross country and participated in track for the past three years at BCHS. He participated in other events, but the high hurdles was the event where he excelled. Bryan stated that track can be a lonely event because you're pretty much on your own with your training table. He said Jeff Lucas did a lot of running with him but on the whole, it's up to you as to how much you train and how serious you are about what you compete in.

Bryan was in good condition this season after competing last season in the semi-state with a bad ankle and a torn tendon. When asked about technique and the methods he used, Bryan said, "I got this book that specialized in the high hurdles and tried to do what it said. You are still on your own once you start to run and you are the one who has to take these hurdles one by one and finish as fast as you can. The first two years there were several injuries where I would miss a hurdle or not get over it right, but these were cut to a minimum this year."

When asked about a track career at Baylor University where Bryan will be attending next year, he said, "No, I won't be doing the hurdles at Baylor. I think I would be too slow. I'll just concentrate on the books." However, Bryan had the concentration to become the best hurdler in conference and region.

BRYAN CHAMBLISS shows the form he used to set a new conference mark of 16.3 in the 120 yard high hurdles. Bryan also won the region with a 16.2 in the same event at North Bullitt. Last Saturday Bryan again clocked a 16.2 at Richmond, good for a fifth place finish in the semi-state.

Jim Chambliss, above, created "Blind-Sided" after an accident changed his life and awakened a talent for art.

Brain injury opened door to life of art

With each visit to the Fine Arts exhibits at the Kentucky State Fair over the years, I have found myself wishing that I could look on the backs of the paintings, sculptures and photographs and read the stories behind the entries.

There is always a story, you know. In every oil portrait of a tired face; every pencil sketch of a smiling child; in every pair of calloused hands.

Byron Crawford

One of those stories was hidden in the comic, off-balance, self-sculpture of a man in a business suit — titled "Blind-Sided" — that won first place in last year's ceramic sculptures competition, recalled Dennis Shaffner, the fair's fine arts superintendent.

In Vail, Colo., during the summer of 1998, Jim Chambliss was blindsided by a sports utility vehicle as the 34-year-old walked across a parking lot near his home, Shaffner said. The Hardinsburg, Ky., native was a successful lawyer with degrees from Transylvania University and the University of Denver School of Law.

The accident did not even knock him off his feet. Though his head had snapped against the SUV when he was struck, he was diagnosed with only a mild concussion.

In the months that followed, however, he would pass out and wake up in intensive care with partial amnesia; lose consciousness and wreck his car; then notice he was losing his vocabulary and suffering serious memory lapses.

The diagnosis was temporal lobe epilepsy. The left side of his brain had been damaged by what seemed a harmless bump. Eventually, unable to drive for 5 ½ years or to continue his law practice — and nearly broke from medical expenses — he took a job substitute teaching.

Then something amazing happened. Jim Chambliss developed a talent for art.

"I was playing around with a block of Styrofoam one day while working as a substitute teacher, and carved a salamander from memories of my childhood that impressed the students and faculty at the high school," he recalled.

Shifting sides of his brain

It was as if the damaged left side of his brain had somehow shifted focus to an enhanced right-brain concentration on a hidden talent for artistic expression.

By 2001, with help from his neuropsychologist, family and friends, the Brain Injury Trust and vocational rehabilitation, he had enrolled in art school at the University of Louisville, from which he earned a master's degree.

Although his work has since earned several awards and international recognition, his Kentucky State Fair first-place award for the self-sculpture inspired by his brain injury marked a memorable transformation from lawyer to artist for Jim Chambliss.

And it has reinforced his passion for unraveling part of the complex mystery of how injured brains often awaken a sleeping gift of artistic creativity.

Now, with a prestigious International Postgraduate Research Scholarship to the University of Melbourne, Chambliss is working toward a combined doctorate in creative art and medicine.

His ongoing research into the influence of epilepsy, bi-polar conditions, multiple sclerosis and other brain disorders on art has become more than an academic pursuit.

"I feel compelled to help others in similar circumstances," he said. "I want to use my art, research and experiences to serve as a catalyst to promote further research."

Chambliss hopes to expand his research to the United States and plans to invite many artists in the Kentucky State Fair arts competition to participate in some of his studies.

Behind every piece at the Kentucky State Fair, there is a story.

Byron Crawford's column appears on the Metro page Sundays, Wednesdays and Fridays. You can reach him at (502) 582-4791 or e-mail him at bcrawford@courier-journal.com. You can also read his columns at www.courier-journal.com.

Doc and Boys at Brad's wedding
Bryan - Brad - Doc and Jim

LAWYER / ARTIST & DOCTOR / TEACHER

"Best Friends"
Jim: Lawyer, Artist, Author, Researcher and PhD - Art and Medicine
Bryan: Psychiatrist, Medical School Professor, Writer

Bryan Chambliss
Baylor University

Jim Chambliss
TransylvaniaUniversity

To Brad Chambliss With best wishes, Ronald Reagan

Brad Chambliss
National Vice President Future Farmers of America
University of Kentucky

To Brad Chambliss
With best wishes, *Gg Bush*

Brad Chambliss
National Vice President
Future Farmers of America
Making a presentation to President George Bush

Jim Chambliss bungee jumping off world's highest suspension bridge in New Zealand

Jim Chambliss, standing rafting guide down the Colorado River

Jim Chambliss reward for hours of practice

Brad and Carla Chambliss with Clay and one of their many Champions.

Brad's four sons' first day of school
Front to back: Caleb, Clint, Clay and Cooper, unhappy at being left behind

Australian grandchildren
Zac and Chloe

Zac Chambliss

Four granddaughters
Lucy - Zoe - Maddie - Chloe

CHAPTER 18

Things I Have Learned and Want to Pass Along to My Sons and Others

There is an old Scottish proverb that says "Open confession is good for the soul." Confession is definitely a Biblical teaching.

I have always been a very private person, and public confession has not been my practice. I do all my confessing privately to God on a daily basis, for which He has promised forgiveness – if we are humble and sincere.

I wrote a book in the late '70s entitled *What I Want to Tell My Boys*. I gave them a copy but never had it published. In mid-life, I experienced a series of setbacks that disappointed me and discouraged me from carrying through with my plans. At one time, I didn't think I was worthy to give advice or serve as a role model. I gradually worked my way through it, with God's love and forgiveness. I feel--and prayerfully hope—that it will be appropriate now, despite the deficiencies of its author. We all have our problems.

Maybe this country boy with more than fifty-three years' experience practicing medicine and the healing arts in a cross-section of our society can say something that may stimulate thinking. Hopefully, it will be of help to someone. If so, it will have been worth my time to share my thoughts, my life, and my career.

But first *the confession*, or perhaps it could be called *my testimony.* First of all, I recognize that I have lived a blessed life. God has put some incredible people in my life. You have learned, from reading my autobiography in earlier chapters, that I had the best possible start. I recognize that, and I am eternally grateful for it. With proper and exceptional early nurturing and training, I accepted Jesus Christ as my personal Lord and Savior at age nine. From the start, I consulted with God on every personal decision through prayer, studying the Bible, and talking to wise and mature Christians.

I even prayed that He would send me a dedicated, devoted Christian wife, and He did (pretty, too!). I have spoken and written volumes about her already and can't praise her enough. I am thankful to God for her.

I prayed for three children, and we were given three fine, exceptional sons of whom I am very proud, as you can see by what I have written and, no doubt, from those who know me personally. They all know how I feel about my sons.

God heard my prayers, and early on I consulted Him on everything. I gave Him praise and credit for all my successes. God was good to me, and life was good.

My practice thrived, and since I had the energy, drive, and organizational skills to be as productive as two average physicians, naturally my income was good, and I had extra funds to invest.

Early investments in fast food real estate and banking were good, but eventually had to be sold to cover investments that went bad. A large investment in trucking with my childhood best friend and neighbor, Charlie Robbins, and his father-in-law, C. L. Van Lahr,

President of the First State Bank, was growing faster than we could expand the fleet of tractor trailer trucks. The company had most of the freight operating authority permits (no compete permits) for most of central and western Kentucky. These were lost overnight with a single signature of President Jimmy Carter, who deregulated the trucking industry in 1980. Profit was no longer possible, and the company was eventually sold at considerable loss.

The biggest loss, however, came from a farming operation I loved, which got too big – too fast. I wanted to put together one of the best registered Hereford operations in the United States. At one time we had over 1000 head of cows and calves. The cattle market went into an uninterrupted ten-year down cycle, and we lost everything, including our beloved family farm that had been purchased and paid for in full from my parents. It broke my heart! My father had trusted me with the preservation of the family farm. We were able to keep and still live in our dream house on the hill and still enjoy the surrounding pastoral scenes and cattle grazing in the fields.

You note I said "I wanted." I had gradually stopped consulting with God on everything and over a period of time, gradually started thinking those earlier successes were because of my own "smarts." Proverbs 16:18 says, "Pride goeth before the fall." The Bible plainly teaches that pride is the sin that God hates most.

At one time my liabilities greatly exceeded my assets. The good full-time cattle farmers in America with manageable debt or no debt survived this down cycle in the cattle market. Many of us didn't, especially among purebred cattle breeders.

I had the option to declare bankruptcy and start all over. I was advised to declare bankruptcy. Many full-time, part-time, or hobby farmers did just that during that time. I said, "No! I made the debt, and I will work until I pay if off." By tightening my belt, driving the same car for thirteen years, taking very few days off, and working hard, with the help of God--I'm getting close. I have no regrets over the hard work, because that is what I enjoy most on this earth anyway. I do regret being unable to give as generously to the church and others as I once did.

I asked God to forgive me for leaving Him out of my life and returned to my previous dedication working for "His church and His kingdom on earth." I once again went back to depending on Him, living for Him with an *attitude of gratitude*. Currently I am close to completing all my obligations and, hopefully, no local bank or lender will have to pay for my mistakes. My local banker is also a respected friend and stayed with me until I paid the bank in full. I thank him, and I thank God for His many random acts of kindness. I have enjoyed immensely the past twenty years working hard for our local church, where I have had the privilege of serving as a deacon for forty-eight years and teaching Sunday School for over forty years. I have also served in the Gideon ministry over twenty years. One of the functions of the Gideon ministry, as many of you know, is to collect money to purchase Bibles that are distributed worldwide. The other function is personal witness. I am back to my earlier commitment and dedication to Him and following His command to "love God, love your neighbor as yourself, and to serve Him."

He has blessed our local church with a beautiful new facility on the bypass and with a greater desire by our church to serve our community. To God be the glory! I am only one of many who dedicated energy and resources to make this possible. I love my church and my church family.

So what has all this taught me? First and foremost, don't ever leave God out of your life.

Second, family is more important than being a physician (or anything). Family is more important than accumulating wealth. Why? The very destiny and future of our country depends upon the character, ethics, and morality we pass on to our families.

Third, dedicate yourself to your primary profession or occupation (this applies to everyone but especially to young physicians). If you are a young physician, acquire all the medical knowledge you can. Be the best you can be at what you have chosen as your life's work and dedicate all your time to that. *Get professional help to manage your investments and retirement.*

Fourth, remember – God is good. God is fair. God loves us like the adopted children we are, but we have to live life His way! He will provide for His own. King Solomon, the wisest man who ever lived, came to this conclusion after trying everything "under the sun." In Ecclesiastes 12:13 he says, "Let us hear the conclusion of the whole matter. Fear (have reverence for) God. and keep His commandments; for this is the whole duty of man."

Remember, as a recent gospel song written and sung by Bill Gaither and Larry Gatlin proclaims, we followers of Christ are…

> "…*greatly blessed*
> *highly favored*
> *imperfect, but*
> *forgiven children of God!*"

God promises in the Bible that believers will be "joint heirs with Christ".."

Can you imagine that?

Think about it!

Prioritize your life, which means putting first things first:

God

Family

Country (community)

Profession or occupation

All the rest (basketball fits in here somewhere).

Written for my children and grandchildren and yours, for thoughtful consideration.

Janet and I love you all and greatly desire to spend eternity with you.

CHAPTER 19

The Beginning of the End

On November 11, 2011, I went to the doctor – a neurologist I had been referring patients to for years. I was pretty sure I knew what was going on. I had developed an occasional tremor around my mouth. I had never seen anyone in my family do that, so I questioned it being a benign familial (essential) tremor.

Dr. Meckler examined me thoroughly and said, "Bob, you have early signs of Parkinson's disease." I had already made a self-diagnosis, as family practice doctors are prone to do. Coming from the mouth of a prominent neurologist, however, it somehow sounded different and more definite! More ominous!

As all family practice doctors, I have had considerable experience in treating Parkinson's disease and this I knew for sure: Parkinson's disease is incurable! Parkinson's disease is progressive! Parkinson's disease is disabling! Parkinson's disease can lead to dementia! Nursing homes are full of patients with Parkinson's disease!

On the positive side, I knew that usually the later in life you develop Parkinson's disease, the slower it progresses. Usually, but not always! I was starting with Parkinson's disease late in life. Having reached the age of seventy-three at that time and being diagnosed with Parkinson's disease, I knew I had arrived at the "fourth quarter."

In basketball I have always loved the fourth quarter, because the fourth quarter is where the action is! The fourth quarter is where the most excitement is, where heroes are made, championships are won, and legends are born. In the fourth quarter, you get the most applause, with people on their feet cheering you on. It is in the fourth quarter that coaches play their most experienced players. It is in the fourth quarter that players play hurt, playing with pain and calling on their last bit of energy. Winners love the fourth quarter so much and victory so much that they are willing to *leave it all on the floor* for the good of the team. In the fourth quarter, experienced players know that victory is never achieved without teamwork.

I prayed to God that He would allow me to have a good "fourth quarter," playing hurt with grit, fortitude, determination, courage, dignity, strength of character, and as much sense of purpose as I could muster.

Teamwork would be needed more than ever. I have a wife that I can always count on to go the extra mile for me, despite the fact that she has her own problems now. After noting some left-sided weakness, she was diagnosed with a large brain tumor in September of 2007. A biopsy was done showing a meningioma, fortunately benign. The tumor, however, was located close to the part of her brain that controls the left side of her body, so we elected to radiate the tumor and shrink it rather than do surgery and run the risk of paralyzing her left side. This was done successfully.

In 2016, a large cyst developed alongside the meningioma, again causing some increased weakness of her left arm and leg. On June 22, 2016 she had brain surgery with removal of part of the cyst and meningioma in addition to a shunting procedure.

Following the surgery, she had temporary paralysis of her left side. Her arm returned to normal in a few days, but she was left with weakness of her left leg including a left foot drop for which she has to wear a brace and take physical therapy (now going on ten months). As one would predict, she has dedicated herself to it completely and is walking without a brace, walker, or cane and is back to her normal routine taking care of me.

During this time, we had a complete role reversal with me being the nurse and helping with the meals and housework. Everyone has been amazed by her determination to improve and return to normal, but knowing her willpower, I predicted that she would. As always, she is more concerned about me.

I have an office staff that has promised to stay with me and be honest with me if my skills begin to decline. Remember, one of the duties of a physician is to do no harm. They promised to "cover my back" (and my patients).

I have physician specialists (friends of mine) who make sure I get the best medical care (they may be a little overly cautious with multiple extensive tests. I forgive them!).

I have a practice that is loyal and encourages me to keep practicing medicine. They cheer me on! Several of them have gone so far as to say, "Doctor, please live longer than I do!"

I have a family that will support me in any way and every way possible. I have close church and minister friends who pray for me daily.

I attended a Parkinson's disease support group at Norton Suburban Hospital in Louisville, Kentucky and was encouraged by other physicians who have been practicing medicine, even surgery, for ten years after they were initially diagnosed.

I have a nephew-in-law who is a retired Air Force colonel who has been brought back from the brink with DBS surgery (deep brain stimulation) and is living a good life in retirement, walking normally with minimal tremor. So that encourages me.

I have an excellent neurologist who said to me on November 11, 2011, "Bob, here is the game plan. My philosophy is to hit Parkinson's disease early and hit it hard. We will make adjustments as we go along, and since I know it is your objective to practice medicine as long as you can, our goal will be to keep you functional as long as we can. Knowing your personality, I know I will get your best effort in maximizing pharmaceutical treatment, physical therapy, and increased rest."

Since I had already worked fifteen years full time with a five-vessel coronary artery bypass that usually lasts ten years, I knew my heart would probably be my limiting factor for longevity – not the Parkinson's disease. However, I recently had a left heart catheterization which showed the five bypasses to be wide open, for which I am grateful.

So far, the "fourth quarter" has been challenging, but rewarding. Cutting back has been the hardest thing. Experiencing long time treasured patients and friends transfer their care to younger providers has hurt the most, even though I realize that I cannot take care of the number of patients I have in the past. My prayer is that I can turn in a winning or at least an above-average performance. God willing – I will keep making a contribution to my family, my patients, my church, and my community.

I will face the end of the game with as much courage as I can. As we say in basketball, I will try to "leave it all on the floor." I am determined not to feel sorry for myself. For my wife's sake, I will try not to be too grumpy. I will try to be independent, taking care of myself as long as I can, so I can take care of her and my patients as long as possible.

As for the end of the game, I know how it comes out. I have already won the game! God has promised eternal life to all who believe. I BELIEVE.

Until that day, God willing, I will continue to make a contribution and *count my blessings.* (See Appendix D- 365 days of Counting My Blessings.) Until that day, I will push on. Like the speaker in Robert Frost's poem, "Stopping by the Woods on a Snowy Evening," I have miles and miles to go before I sleep.

My not-so-secret ambition is to practice medicine in my home county of Breckinridge County for fifty years. That date would be June 29, 2019.

CHAPTER 20

Epilogue

WHAT DIFFERENCE DOES IT MAKE?

This book begins with a nine-year-old boy planning his future and continues with him living it out with some success and some failures. It ends with a grandson planning his future, which I predict will provide him with both success and failures. Both will mold him into the person God has planned for him to be and help him fulfill God's purpose for his life. To be sure, God does have a purpose for his life, for which he was created. He will discover what that is. My prayer is that when God opens doors, my grandson will walk through – excited and unafraid, because one life can make all the difference in the world. The same goes for all our nine grandchildren (and yours).

What difference does it make?

It determines the very character of our nation. It determines what kind of world we will leave for our children and grandchildren. It determines the future prosperity of our country. It determines the resiliency of our democracy and the determination of our nation to hold on to the truth that should be self-evident, "that all men are created equal, that they are endowed by their creator with certain unalienable rights, that among those are life, liberty, and the pursuit of happiness." Collectively it controls the destiny of our nation.

It is achieved by loving God and loving each other. It is achieved by loving and sharing the good life with our family and friends and working through the hard times with our family and community.

Every life does make a difference!

Mine and yours!

I will end this book with two family stories to illustrate how a family should function. One is about my brother, Paul (deceased), and the other about a grandson namesake just getting his life started.

First, however, I would like to say a few words about my family. I have had the privilege to be physician to my entire family, which covers five generations: grandparent, parents, brothers and sisters, their children and grandchildren, nieces and nephews, and many aunts, uncles, and cousins. Add to this most of my in-laws who live nearby.

They have honored me with their respect and trust. Many of their families have asked me to deliver eulogies at their funerals, and I did each one I was asked to do.

My immediate family is huge, at times up to 75-80 living members. We have had, until recent years, a family reunion every two years at Janet's and my house, which is on the family farm up on the hill behind my parents' home.

The first story is about my brother, Paul. Paul was one of the most unusual of the clan, and my other seven brothers and sisters were all motivated to come home every reunion to "check on Paul." Some came more often. This covered a period of forty years.

Paul suffered from a bipolar disorder (manic-depressive illness), and when he was in his manic phase he was hilarious with his wit and charm, much like Jonathan Winters, and many other great comedians who have had a similar problem.

When Paul was occasionally at the other extreme emotionally, he would run away from home, starting as a teenager and continuing most of his life. My parents, with the help of the police, would issue an APB, and with their help would always find him somewhere in the USA, and we would go retrieve him. Once I flew to Detroit to bring him home.

My mother, who had rheumatic heart disease, literally willed herself to live another ten years (to age eighty-eight) because she felt Paul needed her. When Mom died, Janet and I continued to look after him. He continued to live in the farm homestead at the foot of the hill as long as he could. He ate most of his meals at a local restaurant where most of the "retired men" hang out, and I would go in each month and take care of the charges. Everyone loved Paul. The restaurant workers and his many, many friends contributed to his care.

His malady held our family together for all those years just as Dr. O'Connor, my psychiatrist friend, predicted it would. Everyone was happy to do their part. Fortunately, he had a loving and caring family.

I did his eulogy (which follows). I entitled it "My Brother's Keeper." This eulogy helps answer these often-asked questions: What difference does a caring family make? What difference does a caring physician make? *We all need each other. Sometimes it's your turn – sometimes it is mine.* Joe Miller, my good friend, likes this quote.

EULOGY TO PAUL CHAMBLISS
by Bob Chambliss

"And the Lord said unto Cain, 'Where is Abel thy brother?'" And he said, "'I know not; am I my brother's keeper?'" (Genesis 4:9)

This morning I will try to answer that time-honored question for the Chambliss family. We are gathered here today to celebrate the life of Paul Chambliss, who was a most unique creation of God.

Paul brought laughter to the Chambliss family. Many of the Chamblisses are way too serious – Lillian, Jack, and I, to name a few. We have needed Paul's laughter. Even Mom, the most serious of the lot, would laugh through her tears at some of Paul's wit and antics.

Paul told his friends at Cova's Restaurant about his family. "Jack," he said, "works way too hard. Bob is working himself to death. I average the family out." Everyone in the restaurant laughed heartily. When it came to laughter, Paul also averaged the family out, but on this issue he led the curve. Paul had the unique ability to make people laugh. He had more friends and fewer enemies than anyone I have ever known. There isn't a person here today that doesn't have a funny "Paul story" or "Herk story," and many of you have shared your stories with us this weekend; we have enjoyed them and appreciate it.

Everyone who knew Paul liked him, and we never worried about Paul getting sick or lost in this community, because his many friends would come to his rescue and report back to us or bring him home. They did so many times.

To the many restaurant workers and friends (many here today) the Chambliss family wants to say "Thank you." We appreciate you so much. You adopted Paul as part of your family and took care of him like one of your very own. Only in a small community could this be possible.

Paul doesn't have a long résumé to review here today. He doesn't have a long list of accomplishments. He doesn't have a successful career to point to. Paul, you see, had to live his life with a mental disease known as bi-polar disorder – a very complicated problem. I am not ashamed to state this publicly. It was the hand Paul was dealt, and he had to live with it. He did remarkably well, much better than most. In the words of Mom Chambliss, "He did the very best he could do under the circumstances."

My father never understood bipolar disorder. Dad was a very straight-laced person who thought anyone could do right – _if they wanted to._ He didn't understand Paul, but he never gave up on him and often said he would give his life's earnings to make Paul well.

One day Paul and two of his friends, whose names I won't divulge, had been partying a bit too much and decided they would operate on Paul's tom cat to keep it from prowling the neighborhood every night. They went to Taylor's Pharmacy and got some chloroform from their friend, Bobby Neil Taylor, the pharmacist's son and future pharmacist, and put the cat to sleep. Halfway through the procedure, the cat suddenly woke up, ran straight up the outside of the back of our house, latched on to an upstairs window screen with all four feet, and squalled as loud as a cat can squall for five minutes. Dad hollered out through the kitchen window, "Paul Wilton, what's wrong with that cat?" And Paul replied, "I don't know, Dad. It's been acting strange here lately."

When things were serious, it was Paul Wilton. To sister Mabel, it was Paulie. To most of us, Paul. To most of you, Herk. How do you get a name like Herk? In grade school Paul was very skinny but declared he could hold his own against anybody. His classmates asked how he thought he could do that. He flexed his skinny muscles and said, "Because I have hidden powers – like Hercules!" The name Herk stuck.

As a youngster, Paul was bright, intelligent, fun-loving, witty, and charming – the life of the party. I once remarked to Paul's psychiatrist, a friend of mine, that it was such a tragedy that Paul, who had the highest IQ of all the Chambliss family, was wasting his life. He scolded me immediately and told me never to say that again. He said something I will never forget "Handicapped people like Paul are important and vital in our society. They teach us how to love. They teach us how to be grateful for our personal blessings, and they keep families together." (Every life makes a difference!)

I've thought about that often – "They keep families together." Our family is very close, although spread out all over the USA. They come and go frequently, and we have a huge family reunion every two years. Since the death of Mom and Dad years ago, the family has continued to come home because everyone has wanted to touch base with Paul.

Every brother and sister and in-law in the family has contributed regularly to Paul's upkeep. A sister-in-law, Doris Chambliss, was sitting with Paul at Norton's Hospital the night he died, and we love you for that, Doris. Janet, as you know, has been Paul's substitute mom since Mom died and did all the "Mamma things," as Brad says, for Paul. Paul would always say, "Janet, you are a good girl." Linda Holloway, my office manager, paid all of Paul's bills and helped with his correspondence. (Linda, Paul thought you were special.)

I've heard the older nieces and nephews say to the younger ones that it is a shame that they didn't know Paul before his personality was blunted by electric shock treatments and forty years of Thorazine and Lithium. He loved children, and they loved him and thought he was the most fun of all the Chamblisses. He loved to tease them, and he especially loved to tease Grandma Lyons, who lived with us from time to time. Paul came in one day from town and said, "Grandma, I just heard they have thrown Corinth Baptist Church [her church] out of the Association." Grandma, who had no sense of humor, reacted as Paul calculated she would, to Paul's delight.

Paul's reputation extended beyond Breckinridge County. Mr. Gabe of Gabe's Restaurant and Hotel in Owensboro, Kentucky, asked one of our citizens if he knew Paul Chambliss. He did. Mr. Gabe related this story. One day Paul wandered into Gabe's Restaurant, barefoot, both pant legs rolled up to the knees, and a minnow bucket in hand. He walked over to the ballroom piano, set the minnow bucket on the baby grand piano and sat down and started playing, singing little ditties and limericks, and cracking jokes. People gathered around, and Mr. Gabe said it was the best entertainment that had ever been provided at Gabe's Restaurant in his memory. After thirty minutes, Paul picked up his minnow bucket and made one of his famous rapid exits, never to be seen again.

Paul's résumé is not too long, but his character traits are. Paul had a great sense of humor, as we have discussed. Paul was a grateful person.

Because of circumstances, he had to receive more than he could give, but he was always so appreciative. He never failed to thank me for everything I ever did for him, and he never forgot it.

Paul was loyal – loyal to his family and loyal to his friends. If every patient had as much faith in me as Paul did, my practice would be a huge success. He thought I could fix any problem. During the last twenty years of his life, he depended on me for every need and every decision – much like a child depends on his parents. He would come in the back door of the office and slip up to me wherever I was and start to tell me about whatever part of his anatomy that wasn't working right – regardless of what it was and oblivious to whoever might be around. I would say, "Paul, let's step inside this empty exam room and talk about it."

He called his doctor "Bobby." His friends at the restaurant were always amused about his references to his doctor Bobby. After his heart attack, one day he announced he was going to see Bobby, and when he came back from the office to the restaurant they said, "Well, what did Bobby say?" Paul, not to be outdone, said, "He said I should smoke two packs of cigarettes and drink six beers every day."

My security was Paul's security. He was always concerned about my welfare, and whenever he heard something unkind about me at the restaurant he would worry about it until I assured him it was ok – usually not exactly like he had heard it. If it was just exactly like he heard it – it would hurt him. He was my greatest booster, and he was proud of me and all the seventy-five or eighty of us in the Chambliss clan.

Paul was honest and trustworthy. He loved to tease but he never shaded the truth. He told it exactly like it is.

Paul was a gentleman and respectful to all who deserved respect.

Paul was humble and kind and caring and tender-hearted. He loved animals and especially baby animals and kept the farm covered up with cats and dogs and goats and geese and swans and peacocks.

Paul loved his mother, and his mother loved him unconditionally with all her heart. The last thing Mom said to me was, "Bob, take care of Paul." I once asked Mom, "Which of your eleven children do *you love the most?" She said, "I will answer like Charles Wesley's mother when she was asked the same thing about her nineteen children. 'I love the one who is sick until he is well. I love the one who is lost until he comes home.'" Mom said, "Read Luke 15:3" which I have marked in my Bible as <u>Mom's verse</u>. "If you had 100 sheep and one of them strayed away and was lost in the wilderness, wouldn't you leave the ninety-nine others and go and search for the lost one until you found it?"*

Mom taught the Chambliss clan well on being your brother's keeper. The Apostle John addressed the issue in 1 John 4. In verses 17 and 18 he said, "If someone who is supposed to be a Christian has money enough to live well and sees a brother in need and won't help him, how can God's love be within him? Little children, (fellow Christians) let us stop just saying we love people, let us really love them and show it by our actions."

I trust the Chambliss family has shown its love by their actions.

PAUL HAS TAUGHT US HOW TO BE OUR BROTHER'S KEEPER.
He hasn't been heavy – he is our brother and I'm proud of him.

The second story is about Clint Robert Chambliss, Brad and Carla's second of four sons, a sixth-grade student at the T.K. Stone School in Elizabethtown, Kentucky. Clint was one of the sixteen winners out of three hundred and fifty entries in the 2016 Magnolia Bank – <u>Preparing for Success Essay</u> writing contest. Clint entitled his essay "The Doctor" and revealed his desire to become a physician.

It is humbling and gratifying to have a grandson and namesake want to follow in your footsteps. I will end my book with a quote from Clint's essay entitled "The Doctor," expressing his aspiration to spend his life "helping people get back on track with life." (His essay is at the end of this chapter).

For fifty-three years, "helping people get back on track with life" is what this country doctor has been doing and wants to keep on doing as long as I have enough strength and sound mind to do it. Clint nailed it!

For the past twenty years, I have been asked over and over when I was going to retire. My answer has always been the same: "When I fall over" or "When God decides."

My choice is to keep on with Clint's ambition – "to help people get back on track with their lives." I have loved every minute of it. I love my patients, and I love my staff.

CLINT'S ESSAY:
(6th grade – 2016)
BANK OF MAGNOLIA
PREPARING FOR SUCCESS ESSAY

THE DOCTOR
By Clint Chambliss

What makes a great career? What makes a career is one that runs in your family, one that makes you strive to improve, something that is not a job, it is your witness and your calling. This is why I want to be a doctor. My grandfather is a doctor, my uncle is a doctor, and I have always loved to find out how the human body works. One day I could be the one to cure cancer or a new disease that threatens humankind's existence.

The best place to help me follow my dreams is the University Vanderbilt. In addition, my grandfather graduated from Vanderbilt to get his medical degree. It takes four years for a basic degree, but to get a master's or doctorate it takes longer. It would be a great honor to follow my grandfather's steps, to participate and share in his dream. To help me to be ready for Vanderbilt, I am taking extra science and math in high school.

There are many people like my grandfather who opened a clinic in Hardinsburg or anywhere because they love "<u>helping people get back on track with life</u>." That is what I want to do. I can make my own clinic or take over my grandfather's clinic. I could make 100k-500k doing what inspires me. Whether I can chase this dream has not been decided, but I will do all I can to make the doors open for my future.

P.S. From the grandfather. I treasure Clint's statement, "<u>It is your witness and your calling</u>." This is very mature thinking for a twelve-year-old. I tear up every time I read this! I think it adds an exclamation point to my life and my career!

THAT IS THE DIFFERENCE IT MAKES!

I hope my epitaph reads:
HIS LIFE MADE A DIFFERENCE.

ONE OF MY FAVORITE SONGS
PRECIOUS MEMORIES

Precious Memories, unseen angels
Sent from somewhere to my soul.
How they linger, ever near me
And the sacred past unfold.

Precious Father, Loving Mother
Fly across the lonely years,
And old home scenes of my childhood
In fond memories appear.

In the stillness of the midnight
Echoes from the past I hear
Old time singing, gladness bringing
From the lovely land somewhere.

As I travel on life's pathway
Know not what the years may hold
As I ponder hope grows fonder
Precious Memories flood my soul.

Precious Memories, how they linger
How they ever flood my soul
In the stillness of the midnight
Precious sacred scenes unfold.

Clint Robert Chambliss - 6ᵗʰ grade
3ʳᵈ generation Robert who aspires to become a 3ʳᵈ generation physician

Dr. Chambliss vacationing in Hawaii

Bob and Janet Chambliss - Golden years

APPENDIX A

I. A Physician's Day Book

APRIL 6, 1964 AND JUNE 30, 1969

First Day In

CUMBERLAND COUNTY

PHYSICIAN'S DAY BOOK

Date April 6, 1964

	NAME AND ADDRESS	SERVICES RENDERED	INCOME
1	_____ O.C.	3.00	— ✓
2	_____ O.C.	3.00	— ✓
3	O.V.	3.00	3.00
4	O.V. MC	3.00	— ✓
5	O.V.	3.00	3.00
6	O.V.	3.00	3.00
7	O.V. Family MC	8.00	— ✓
8	O.V.	3.00	3.00
9	O.V. ea. MC	6.00	— ✓
10 Lunch	O.V. MC	3.00	— ✓
11	O.V.	3.00	— ✓
12	O.V.	3.00	3.00
13	O.V	3.00	3.00
14	O.V. + inj. MC	4.00	1.00
15	O.V. + inj MC	4.00	— ✓
16	Sutures of Chin	15.00	5.00 ✓
17	Home Call	9.00	9.00
18	O.V. (night)	4.00	— ✓
19	Paranephric inj. A Lumbarginas	15.00	—

First day in Cumberland County office

| | 98.00 | 35.00 |

FIRST DAY IN BRECKENRIDGE COUNTY

PHYSICIA   30, 1969

First day in Breckenridge County office

#	Services	SERVICES RENDERED	INCOME	
1	not seen	—	—	✓
2	oc, lab, x-ray	16 00	—	✓
3	oc, Inj	6 00	—	✓
4	Inj	1 00	—	✓
5	oc, Inj	6 00	—	✓
6	oc	4 00	4 00	✓
7	oc, Inj	6 00	6 00	✓
8	oc, x-ray	18 00	—	✓
9	oc, UST	5 00	—	✓
10	not seen	—	—	✓
11	oc	4 00	—	✓
12	oc	4 00	—	✓
13	Inj	4 00	—	✓
14	oc, lab, Pap	11 00	9 00	✓
15	VDRL	5 00	—	✓
16	not seen	—	—	✓
17	not seen	—	—	✓
18	not seen	—	—	✓
19	VDRL	5 00	—	✓
20	Exam	8 00	—	✓
21	oc, Inj	6 00	6 00	✓
22	Dressing	4 00	—	✓
23	oc, inj	8 00	—	✓
24	VDRL	5 00	5 00	✓
25	oc, lab	6 00	—	✓
26	script	1 00	1 00	✓
27	oc, exam, lab	7 00	7 00	✓
28	oc, lab	8 00	8 00	✓
29	oc, Inj	10 00	—	✓
30	oc, inj	6 00	6 00	✓
31	oc, EKG	14 00	14 00	✓
32	oc	4 00	4 00	✓
33	oc	4 00	—	✓
34	oc, Inj	6 00	6 00	✓
35	oc, Inj	8 00	—	✓
36	oc, UST	9 00	—	✓
37	oc	8 00	—	✓
38	oc, Inj	6 00	6 00	✓
39	not seen	—	—	✓
		219 00	82 00	

Form No. 13 Copyright 1956 - CLAYSON L. SCROGGINS ASSOCIATES. CINCINNATI. OHIO

	NAME AND ADDRESS	SERVICES RENDERED		INCOME		
40	OC	2	00	2	00	✓
41	OC	4	00	4	00	✓
42	OC	4	00	4	00	✓
43	OC, inj. (2)	8	00	8	00	✓
44	OC, lab	6	00	6	00	✓
45	OB Exam	—		—		✓
46	OC, lab	6	00	6	00	✓
47	OC, inj.	6	00	—		✓
48	NC - H	8	00	—		✓
49	Anesthesia	35	00	—		✓
50	NV - Diam	5	00	—		✓
51	HV - Dism	5	00	—		✓
52	NV -	5	00	—		
53	OC, lab, Pap	11	00	11	00	✓
54	Rec'd on Acc't	—		5	00	✓
55	Rec'd on Acc't (FMC)	—		24	00	✓
56	Rec'd on Acc't (FMC)	—		8	00	✓
57	Rec'd on Acc't (FMC)	—		15	20	✓
58	Rec'd on Acc't (FMC)	—		22	40	✓
59	Rec'd on Acc't (FMC)	—		111	20	✓
60	Rec'd on Acc't (FMC)	—		4	00	✓
61	Rec'd on Acc't (FMC)	—		43	20	✓
62	Rec'd on Acc't (FMC)	—		10	40	✓
63	Rec'd on Acc't (FMC)	—		20	00	✓
64	Rec'd on Acc't (FMC)	—		4	00	✓
65	House Call	8	00	—		✓
66	House Call	8	00	—		✓
67	HV	5	00	—		✓
68	HV	5	00	—		✓
69	HV	5	00	—		✓
70	HV	5	00	—		✓
71	HV	5	10	—		✓
72	HV	5	00	—		✓

II. Hospital Retirement Letter

ROBERT B. CHAMBLISS, M.D.
105 FAIRGROUNDS ROAD
HARDINSBURG, KENTUCKY 40143

September 8, 2014

Dear Hospital Employees, Administration, and Members of the Board of Directors,

After fifty years of getting up at 4:30 a.m. and working a 12+ hour day, I am tired. Many of you have noticed and showed concern, and I appreciate that. Electronic medical records can add more hours, and I am not looking forward to tackling that. It's past time for me to make an adjustment, and I have decided to follow in the footsteps of Dr. Elliott and many primary care providers across America and give up the inpatient part of my practice and turn it over to the hospitalist and other staff members.

I have loved every minute of it – especially the first thirty years – when Dr. Sills and I kept the hospital going, manning the emergency room day and night, and together delivering 300+ babies a year. We kept the hospital profitable all those years.

I have been considering this move for several years – but hated to give it up. Most of my patients will be disappointed, and I regret that. We will all have to adjust to it. It is the current trend in providing medical care.

I want to thank each and every employee of the hospital, past and present, for helping me along the way. I love you all and will miss being pampered. You are all a credit to the hospital, and we are a team – each one important in providing the best care possible for our patients.

It is our job to serve, to love, and to show concern. As you have heard me say many times down through the years, "We should roll out the red carpet for every patient." This makes every patient we serve feel important and appreciated, and it makes them feel secure and optimistic that they will improve. It definitely enhances their speed of recovery. Remember always that we are here to serve the patients, and not for the patient to pad the bottom line for the hospital.

Janet and I thank each and every one of you from the bottom of our hearts.

Sincerely,

Robert B. Chambliss, M.D.
P.S. Have fun every day you work, and serve your patients with joy!

I. I Heard The Silent Hero

Creative Writing by
Bryan Chambliss, 1981

"Bryan, Grandad's dying. The children will be here when we come home from church."

"Dying – how can he be dying? Daddy said that he was doing fine just the other day, Mama."

"I know, Son. That's just the way it happens sometimes."

"Mama, I want to go see Grandad."

"Bryan."

"Yes, Mama?"

"You'll have to prepare yourself for the worst. Grandad doesn't look like the grandfather that you're used to seeing."

"I know that, Mama. But I'm a big boy now. I can handle it."

"Bryan, you've never seen anybody at all in this condition before. It's not a pretty sight."

"I know, Mama. I know. But a man has to see the ugly as well as the pretty. All my life I've seen only the pleasant sights. It's about time that I grow up and see both sides of the world."

"Well, suit yourself. Can you get dressed in time to go to the hospital before we go to Sunday School?"

"Yes, ma'am."

"Then hurry up. And make sure that your room is clean, too. We'll have company before long."

His mother was right. Never in his life had he seen such an unsettling sight. He heard his grandfather laboriously gasping for air. He saw the unnatural thrown-back position of his grandfather's head. Where was the dignity that he had always associated with old age? Why did those awful tubes have to be in his nose? He thought that the tubes seemed to be choking his grandfather. They seemed to pull his head back into a deadly stranglehold, waiting until he would give up and concede the match to his opponent. The youth had never heard his grandfather talk about death, but he did remember his grandfather talking to him about growing old. His grandfather had been watching the youth shoot basketball on a goal in the barn.

"Son, I remember when I used to have that kind of spring in my legs. Someday, you'll lose that spring, also."

"I'm not ever going to get out of shape, Grandad. If I have to, I'll jog even though I might have arthritis in every joint of my body."

"That's the way we all plan to be, Son, but sooner or later age just sneaks up on you and wrestles your strength away. All of a sudden, you find yourself old and feeble, and you have to use a cane to get around."

The youth thought that it was strange to hear his grandfather talk about having to use his cane in order to walk. He had never seen his grandfather's cane as a crutch but rather as a distinguished honor of old age like the weapons that old Indian warriors carried around even though the days in which they used those weapons to become heroes were long past. He considered his grandfather a hero, also--not a glorious hero but a silent one.

Silent heroes receive their glory after death, their memory preserved not in yellowing headlines but in the quiet, lifelong influence they exert on those who know them. His grandfather's life had not been easy, but it was evident from the expression on his face, that look of satisfaction possessed by the quiet warriors in life who are strong enough to overcome life's defeats, that his life had been a good one. His grandfather did not like growing old, but aging was just one of those unpleasant things in life that a man had to accept.

"Bryan."

"Yes, Mama."

"We need to go home and pick up your brothers and father, or we'll be late for church. Are you ready to go?"

"Yes, ma'am. I'm ready."

———❧———

"Did you notice the flowers we sent from you three boys, Bryan?"

"Yes, ma'am. I did. I liked the idea of the Bible with one orchid on it for each one of us boys. Grandad would have liked it, too. His funeral wasn't even very sad, was it? It seemed more like a tribute, like a big dinner in honor of a hero."

"Yes, Son, it was like a tribute because your grandad was a great man. Did you notice that all of your daddy's brothers and sisters at different times slipped away from the crowd to walk through the fields just to be able to think and pray by themselves?"

"Yes, ma'am. I noticed that."

His grandad had loved to walk, and he had loved the Bible. "Always believe the Bible and do what it says, and you'll never be less than a man, Son." That was one of the few things that the youth had ever heard his grandfather say about Christianity. He was a deacon in the church but had always believed that a man's religion was between himself and his God. He took the walks because it gave him an opportunity to talk to God while he was completely alone. His grandfather did everything in a quiet manner. He was one of the silent heroes.

"Where are you going, Son?"

"For a walk, Mama…just goin' for a walk."

A note from his professor at the end of this paper written in class reads:

"This brought tears to my eyes and reminded me of the pain I felt when I lost my grandparents! The content was so good that I got caught up in reading it and didn't notice any structural errors. Would your grandmother enjoy reading this tribute?"

II. Student Commencement Address

UNIVERSITY OF KENTUCKY 1992
BY BRAD CHAMBLISS

*As I look back over all that has happened to me since that eventful day,
I am scarcely able to believe in the reality of my adventures, for they have
been so wonderful that even now I am bewildered when I think of them.*

The words that I have just spoken are not my own, but are the
words of science fictionalist Jules Vern in his novel *Journey to the
Center of the Earth.* They tell the feelings of a young man who has just
traveled many miles, seen many fantastic places; but even more importantly, the journey of which he tells has allowed him to see himself more clearly and to grow as perhaps no other experience could
have allowed him to do. At times, he was awed by his own strength.
But even more often he was humbled by his own weakness, and at his
journey's end he realizes, more than ever, how much he truly owes to
those who have helped him along the way.

No, those were not my words, but they very easily could have
been. It is hard to believe that enough time has passed to allow me
to stand here as a graduate of the University of Kentucky (even
though I am certain that my father disagrees). It seems like only
yesterday that I loaded my 1987 four-wheel-drive Chevy Scottsdale
pick-up truck with my nicely pressed clothes, an extra pair of ten-
nis shoes, the thirty towels I got for graduation, and a two-year-old
unused electric razor and headed east on the Bluegrass Parkway
to Lexington. I will never be able to shake from my memory the
contrast of emotions I had on that drive. I was overwhelmed by

feelings of both uncertainty and optimism. As I stand here today, I am certain I was not alone with those feelings as an incoming freshman, or now as a graduating senior. Today as each of us complete our college tenure and prepare ourselves for a successful entry into the work force or a post-graduate education, we leave this institution with those same feelings of optimism and uncertainty.

Our feelings of uncertainty are justified, not only because we are completing our adventures as college students and starting anew on another of life's wonderful journeys, but because we live in an era where it is easy for us to become doubtful or even cynical or despondent about what our future holds, especially when we are continually bombarded with facts and figures telling us that America has lost its competitive edge. We listen to critics both at home and abroad telling us that America, long the envy of the world, is on the slippery slope of decline; that with her racial tensions, violent streets, drug addictions, and homelessness she is no longer the beckoning place she once was. These uncertainties leave us wondering; could America really be arriving at the end of a long and glorious period of prosperity and world leadership?

Not a chance! Our journeys have only started. Our country today stands poised with as much potential as the nation of our forefathers. It is true our nation faces colossal problems, but these challenges are no greater than those faced by our forefathers, and I am confident that we are no less innovative, no less inventive, and no less concerned than they. I am convinced that if this nation is to be no more, it won't be because of overwhelming external challenges created by change, but because we internally failed to adapt to them. Our history abounds with great achievements in the face of crisis and adversity that has allowed America to become the most blessed of all nations, but we must never allow ourselves as a nation or as individuals to believe we have arrived at true greatness. For if we do not continue to move forward with a vision of future greatness and an unyielding commitment to translate that vision into reality, we will surely become only an obsolete remnant of the past.

We must readily admit that the challenges our nation faces are real and no matter how great a nation, institution, or cause, it is only one generation away from extinction. Our nation cannot afford a generation of mere symbolic leadership. It demands a generation of values-driven crusaders who realize that the true purpose of their education is not just a continual accumulation of knowledge and skills, but a preparation for action and service.

No, we have not arrived. There is still much work to be done. As long as someone cannot look to the future with hope because of the color of their skin or sex or socio-economic status – we have not arrived... as long as someone lies dying in a hospital bed with AIDS or cannot simply afford proper medical care – we have not arrived...as long as kids cannot learn because of violence or drugs in their school – we have not arrived... as long as any American's individual rights and freedoms are being suppressed – we have not arrived.

Our nation is yearning for political, business, and educational leaders who are ready to realistically address the challenges of today and tomorrow, realizing that to be successful in today's progressive society, we must be a new breed endowed with the quality of adaptation, the ability to accept the inevitable, to conform to the unavoidable, to harmonize with rapidly changing conditions, but most importantly, possessing the courage to travel down new and unexplored roads armed with nothing but our own knowledge and vision.

The direction we will take will ultimately be left to discussion and debate. Our participation, however, in the future of this commonwealth and nation is non-negotiable. I grant that in the words of Robert F. Kennedy, there is little that one man or woman can do against the enormous array of the world's ills, against misery and ignorance, injustice and violence. Few will have the greatness to bend history itself, but each of us must strive to change a small portion of events, and in the totality of those acts shall be written the history of this generation. History will be written by those individuals who dream of the impossible and strive to achieve it, and in so doing they will raise the stature of man a fraction of an inch in the process, whether it is an aspiration achieved or not.

As we look back on what has occurred during our academic careers, we have seen events unfold that have changed the complexion of the entire world. Years from now, when our time to serve has come and gone, and our children and their children reflect on what we have done, what images will they see? What contribution will we have made? My greatest fear is that in my lifetime I will not have used my God-given talents and abilities, no matter how limited, to their ultimate potential.

Within this room lie many of the answers to the challenges of this and future generations, but will we meet those challenges? There are no guarantees, no entitlements, and no limitations to what we can achieve. So, let us begin. Let us begin, knowing that as we travel on our individual journeys we will at times be humbled by our own individual weaknesses and at times awed by our own individual strengths, but if we travel together with a vision of future generations and an unyielding commitment to translate that vision into reality, we can truly change the world. We cannot be certain of what our future holds, but we can rest assured in who holds the future, and in that, we can be confident and unafraid of whatever lies ahead.

Thank you and God bless....

Three Generations
of The Chambliss Family

by Brad Chambliss while at the University of Kentucky

Three Generations of the Chambliss Family

To begin my story, I will have to start with the end of another. It was during the time when millions of Americans were seeing their dreams die as the nation was in the grips of the Great Depression. The year was 1932. During this year my grandparents, Paul Bryan and Elmina Chambliss, saw their dream die, but they also saw the birth of another. It was the year that the Hardinsburg Bank and Trust closed its doors, and my grandparents saw their farm go to the highest bidder. With their farm gone, my grandparents loaded their six children and few belongings into a horse-drawn wagon and moved fifteen miles up the road from McQuady to Hardinsburg, Kentucky. With the financial assistance of my great-uncle Vernon Chambliss, my grandparents made a down payment on a 120-acre farm just outside of town and started building on their new American dream.

They moved into a two-story frame house that had been used by tenant farmers and deserted because of its poor state of repair. My grandmother cried briefly when she saw it but started immediately to transform it into the new home of the Chambliss family. Times were bad then, and I can remember my grandmother saying, "We made a living and that was all." Of course, to my grandmother, a living was just enough to keep the children fed and clothed and hold on to the farm. For the next several years, my grandparents didn't have time to concern themselves with Japan's aggression in the Pacific or Hitler's rise to power. The only thing my grandparents concerned themselves with was the raising of their children in a strong Baptist home, teaching them to appreciate God's good earth, and surviving the Depression.

By 1937 it looked like my grandparents were going to make it out of the red, but it just wasn't meant to be. It was the year of Kentucky's worst flood in history. It was a hard year to make a crop, but after a long summer's work with the corn and fodder and hay safely in the barn along with all of the cattle, the barn caught fire from the overheated fodder, completely destroying the barn and all of the cattle and the year's harvest. To top it all off, in December of that year Robert Bryan Chambliss, my father, was born, making the grand total of children eight and still growing.

The farm economy seemed to turn around in 1939, as did the whole American economy, as our nation unconsciously prepared itself for war. The rural community prospered for the next several years. It was during these years that my grandparents finally paid off the debt owed on their farm. It was also during this time that my grandparents, as well as all farmers, were able to modernize by retiring their old team of mules and purchasing a tractor, along with other effort- and time-saving equipment.

During the war, a farm boy was considered to be aiding the war effort by staying on the farm and had the option of being deferred from serving in the armed forces; however, even with this consideration, I had two uncles who served in the Navy during the war. My Uncle Henry was a welder stationed in Hawaii, and my Uncle Jack was assigned to a mine sweeper in the South Pacific. So, at one point during the war, an American flag with two gold stars on it was proudly exhibited on the front door of my grandparents' two-story white frame house.

After the war, times were good for the Chambliss family. All of the Chambliss men returned home safely, farm prices were good, and Harry S. Truman was president and running for another term. Truman, who was an extremely vocal and outspoken president, was loved by all Breckinridge County, but especially by my grandfather. Both of my parents say they can remember Truman as he made his whistle-stop campaign through Kentucky. They can also remember going to bed the night of the election thinking that Thomas E. Dewey had become our nation's thirtieth president.

Life was simple in rural Kentucky during the fifties, and times were easier for the Chambliss family. Television was in its infancy, and Elvis Presley rocked onto the American scene. Even though the Korean War and the McCarthy Witch Hunts were shocking America, my father, who was attending Breckinridge County High School, concerned himself more with the priorities of a teenager, such as basketball and obtaining a red "James Dean" jacket. Even though the Korean War occurred during my father's teenage years, he still vividly remembers reading in the newspaper the shocking number of fallen Americans and seeing a map of Korea on the front page of the *Courier-Journal* each day with a line across it showing the advancement or withdrawal of the American troops as they fought their way up and down the Korean peninsula.

During the summer of 1958, my grandparents were pleased to be informed that my father was dating a fine upstanding Baptist girl from a neighboring county. There was only one problem with this young lady--she was the daughter of a Republican. Even with this flaw, my father continued to date this young lady, taking her to see movies like *God's Little Acre* and *Ole Yeller*. The following year my father proposed and on June 13, 1959 my father married Janet Sue Bruner of Hawesville, Kentucky.

That fall my father entered Vanderbilt University School of Medicine, having been accepted at the end of his Junior year at the

University of Kentucky. It was during the same time America was helping Fidel Castro rise to power in Cuba that my parents moved to Nashville and closer to the racial problems of the South. After completing his first year of medicine at Vanderbilt, my father decided that he wanted to be a rural family physician and made the decision to transfer to the University of Tennessee Medical School in Memphis – the home of blues music, Elvis Presley, and the Ku Klux Klan.

Even though my father was involved with his studies in medical school and my mother was busy putting my father through school, it was next to impossible to ignore what was going on in America. During the three years my father was in medical school, the nation seemed to be on a roller coaster ride. The ride started with the election of a new energetic and socially attractive president and First Lady from Boston, Massachusetts, but took a quick turn downward as America saw itself getting involved in another nation's political unrest in the Far East as well as the embarrassment of the Bay of Pigs. The ride leveled off with the Cuban Missile Crisis and went upward as the President promised to land a man on the moon. The ride came to an abrupt and tragic end as the nation, and the world, saw its president gunned down on live television. My father recalled the afternoon of the day John F. Kennedy was assassinated, when he returned home from the hospital and turned on the television to see Lady Bird Johnson say her famous words of compassion, "Oh, no! Not in my beloved state of Texas!"

In 1964 my parents moved back to Kentucky for my father to do his internship at Louisville General Hospital. This was the same year President Johnson played on the emotions of Congress concerning the death of John F. Kennedy to get a quicker passage of the Civil Rights Act of 1964 to ensure himself a victory in his election against Senator Barry Goldwater of Arizona. By this time, my mother had quit working to devote her time to my two older brothers—Bryan, who was born while my parents were in Memphis, and Jim, who had just been born at the Jewish Hospital in Louisville, Kentucky.

After completing his internship, my father started his practice in Burkesville in southern Kentucky. From 1965 to 1968, the evening news broadcasts were mostly filled with protest riots and marches. It was in 1968 that "it all seemed to happen." In 1968 the number of riots skyrocketed, the Vietnam conflict (war) escalated, and the Civil Rights Act of 1968 was passed. Martin Luther King and Robert F. Kennedy were assassinated, Nixon was finally elected president, and my grandparents celebrated their fiftieth anniversary and the birth of another grandchild, who happened to be me.

In 1969, only eleven months after I was born, my father moved his practice back home to Hardinsburg and my family back to the family farm. 1969 was an exciting year for my family. I remember my mother saying to me, "You would have thought that your father had flown *Apollo II* to the moon and landed when he first set foot back on the family farm to stay." Even though 1969 was the year of Woodstock and the beginning of the drug culture, the movement didn't seem to directly affect my family or my community.

The early 1970s were the beginning of prosperous days for rural America and the Chambliss family. It was during this time that the Soviet Union and other nations were buying massive amounts of American grain, and the government was encouraging farmers to plant corn from fence row to fence row in order to meet these demands. American farmers were not only reaping larger harvests but larger profits as well. At the same time, the value of land was increasing from 5-15% each year and, even with a narrow profit margin or a streak of bad luck, this inflation made up for a lot of mistakes made by the farmers.

The 1970s will be remembered as the "me" decade. America's attitude during this time may have come from the prosperity it was experiencing and its yearning for more. Traditional moral values were challenged, and America's president was disgraced when he was caught in the "big lie." The most vivid memory I have of the whole Watergate ordeal is when Rich Little made mockery of Nixon by raising both hands in the air in a peace sign and saying, "I am not a crook." I can barely remember Watergate and Nixon's resignation, but I can still hear my parents making the comment that it was a shame that such a good president would lose it all because of such a needless mistake.

In 1976 it seemed like the Chambliss family celebrated all year long. We celebrated my eighth birthday, my grandfather's eightieth birthday, and America's two- hundredth birthday. We also celebrated the election of a Democratic and Southern Baptist President from Plains, Georgia.

The following year I can remember our family keeping their eyes glued to the television set for days and days as we watched the televised *Uncle Tom's Cabin* of the 1970s. Even though *Roots* helped to open the eyes of many Americans about unjust suppression of blacks in our country, racial violence still continued to break out and the Ku Klux Klan membership continued to increase, especially in Kentucky's very own Louisville.

1979 was the beginning of the end of the good times in rural America. Bad times for the American farmer started when President Carter, in protest of the Soviet Union's invasion of Afghanistan, announced the grain embargo and later that year the PIC Program. In 1979 we also saw the American hostages taken in Iran and President Carter's inability to negotiate their return. My family was, however, very pleased when President Carter orchestrated the signing of the Camp David Peace Accord between Egypt and Israel and the signing of the Salt II Treaty with the Soviet Union.

In 1980, however, when Jimmy Carter chose to run for re-election, times were bad and getting worse in Breckinridge County. So, when my parents went to the polls that year, they exercised their right to be Republican-voting Democrats and cast their ballots for Ronald Reagan.

The next four years were hard times for Americans, and my family was no exception, but during the next four years I could see a change in the attitude of our nation that seemed to climax at the 1984 summer Olympic games in Los Angeles, California, as the final torch bearer made his way into the Los Angeles Coliseum around the track and up the steps to light the torch signifying the beginning of the Olympic games. When he lit the flame in the opening ceremonies, it was almost as if he had rekindled the flame of patriotism in the hearts of all Americans that seemed to have been dormant for the previous decade. Times were still bad for many rural Americans, but the warmth of this flame seemed to lessen the pain.

By the end of 1984, inflation had fallen to 4% and unemployment was down to 7%. Ronald Reagan had been elected to four more years, and America seemed well on its way to recovery.

This recovery, however, had not made its way to rural America. Times were still pretty rough in Hardinsburg, Kentucky. Even though my father is a doctor and doesn't depend on farming for his living, he does depend on the farmer. In a rural community, when the farmer hurts, everyone feels the pain, especially in the counties such as Breckinridge County where agriculture is the only industry. This agricultural depression that we are experiencing now has not hit the Chambliss family as hard as it did in 1932, but we are feeling its sting, as are all the residents of Breckinridge County. The Chambliss family will make it through this depression. They will remember the good times and the bad and will always be grateful for the opportunity to live and raise their families in this great country. They will hold true to the best traditions of rural America. They will attempt to be good stewards of the land that has been placed in their hands and pass the land and the traditions on to future generations of the Chambliss family.

Paul and Elmina Chambliss
50th Wedding Anniversary 1968
9 children and 16 of 22 grandchildren
My father on the right behind my mother and new baby (me)
with Bryan and Jim in front on right.

_____ _AMBLISS
_____Ky.

"Attempts the end, and never stands to doubt,

Nothing's so hard but search will find it out."

MECHANICAL AND ELECTRICAL ENGINEERING

Private; Senior Private.
Junior Member A. I. E. E.; Member Engineering Society '18; Cosmopolitan Club; Senior Private Club.

In the fall of 1915 there came to us from "The Hills of Old Kentcky," a lad whom we have all admired and loved, and whom we have known as "Heck." It is in his nature to attack the hardest problems, so we can see why he decided to take the electrical course at Clemson. For three years "Heck" has been a "day cadet;" however, he is one of our most loyal Tigers and his spirit in class and college work is surpassed by none. Oft' times we have been entertained by Heck's recital of jokes and experiences, which shows him to be of a cheerful disposition. Heck firmly believes that tho his home state is noted for pretty girls, he has found one that has the rest beat "all hollow." We have found in Heck a hard worker, a boy of extraordinary individuality, pleasing personality, and steady habits. We predict for him success in all his undertakings.

"We don't know what "lectric'ty's 'bout;
But you bet, BY HECK, we'll soon find out."

SAMUEL PATRICK CLEMONS
Greeleyville, S. C.

"In hearts, steel is more valuable than gold."

AGRONOMY

Corporal; Sergeant; First Sergeant; Senior Sergeant.
Championship Class Football '18; Vice-President Williamsburg County Club '18; President Williamsburg County Club '18, '19; Camp Gordon Club; Senior Non-Com. Club; Y. M. C. A. '16, '17, '18; Promotion Committee '18; Reporting Critic, Literary Critic, Vice-President Palmetto Literary Society; Marshall Society Annual Celebration '18; Winner Declaimer's Medal '17.

"Sammie" claims to hail from Greeleyville, although many of us doubt that such a place exists, but after much exploration we finally located the place. From the beginning he cast his lot with the "Aggies" and has persistently overcome the difficulties and problems of the mysterious science. Aside from his academic duties he has a hobby of admiring musicians, especially of the "fair sex." He confidentially tells us that the height of his ambition is to learn "A Perfect Day." "Sammie" is a strong believer in literary society work and has taken an active part since he came to Clemson. He is to be envied at the ease with which he is able to speak. His "Irish" brogue, constant wit, and everready smile makes him a friend to all. Regardless of what he undertakes, success is sure to crown his efforts, and we can but predict assured happiness and success for this noble son of Greeleyville.

This page was taken from my grandfather's yearbook the year he graduated from Clemson University in 1919. Notice the comments about electricity.

This is my grandmother, Elmina Chambliss, proudly posing for the camera in front of the new homestead in 1939.

The chicken coop was not only a place for chickens but it made an excellent place to play marbles

In 1939 farming was truly a family occupation. As soon as the children were big enough to contribute, they were put to work.

Daddy   Bettye   Haney

Even in 1953, every Kentucky youth dreamed of being a basketball star.

In 1976 my grandfather celebrated his 80th birthday and I celebrated my 8th.

This is my great grandmother's birthplace where grandparents first lived when they moved their family back to Breckinridge County during the Depression. This photo was taken in 1931.
Humble beginnings!

365 Days of Counting My Blessings

COUNTING MY BLESSINGS
ROBERT B. CHAMBLISS, M.D.
2012

Written the year after I was diagnosed with Parkinson's Disease on 11/11/2011

January 1, 2012. After being diagnosed with Parkinson's Disease, I made a New Year's Resolution to daily count my blessings. THESE WILL INCLUDE BLESSINGS GREAT AND SMALL, SOME TRIVIAL, SOME PROFOUND, ALL HEARTFELT. Following the Christmas holidays with all my family at home, I am particularly reminded of what a wonderful family God has given me. A loyal, loving, faithful wife, three fine sons, and nine grandchildren. This is the essence of the good life. I am truly blessed.

January 2. I am blessed to have a Savior who loves me and has provided for my eternal salvation.

January 3. I have been blessed with good health and more energy than anyone should possess. I have some serious health issues recently diagnosed, but will try my best to face them with as much grace and dignity as I can.

January 4. I have been blessed to have had the privilege to practice medicine in my hometown and county among my friends, relatives, and kin – now completing my forty-second year for a total of forty-eight years of medical practice.

January 5. I have been blessed to have had two moral Christian parents who taught us the difference between right and wrong, a good work ethic, family devotion, pride in our country and flag, and that freedom is God-given and success depends on self-motivation and hard work.

January 6. I am thankful for my church family and many there who say I am their mentor and best friend. When I have good fortune or something good happens in my life, they rejoice with me, and when I am in need or ill they pray for me and console me. My church is the center of my life, and I love my church.

January 7. I am blessed to have been born and reared in Hardinsburg, Kentucky, USA. Towns like Hardinsburg, Kentucky are the last best place in the world to live and raise a family.

January 8. I am blessed to have a rural background, tilling the soil, appreciating God's creation, learning a good work ethic at an early age and learning how to be a good neighbor and look out for one another.

January 9. I am thankful for my Sunday School class I have had the privilege to teach for many years, where everyone can honestly share their thoughts and doubts without being judged or criticized. All doubts and different opinions are thrown out on the table for discussion and equally respected. They are all my friends even when we disagree or have a difference of opinion, and everyone feels free to express their true feelings without sugarcoating them.

January 10. I am blessed to have friends who love me even when I am wrong.

January 11. I am blessed to serve a God who gives me a second chance.

January 12. I am blessed to be a good sleeper (most of the time).

January 13. I was blessed as a high school student to have many outstanding teachers and three special mentors to influence me and give me encouragement and direction.

January 14. I am so blessed to have been born in the era of the greatest medical technology in the history of mankind. I am alive because it is possible to do a five-vessel bypass and restore circulation to five vital coronaries that were 95% obstructed. I would not be walking without severe pain except for bilateral knee replacements. My heart may have already stopped were it not for a pacemaker. I could have a severe visual impairment were it not for lens replacements for cataracts. The possibilities go on and on. I am grateful for modern medical technology.

January 15. I am blessed to serve a God who loves me and wants the best for me, who knows my name and thinks about me continuously, who knows my every thought, is patient with me, forgives my sins, and loves me anyway. How's that for amazing grace!

January 16. I am blessed to be an American and live free under our wonderful constitution which guarantees our God given unalienable rights of life, liberty, and the pursuit of happiness, as stated in the Declaration of Independence. My prayer is that we can pass it on to our grandchildren.

January 17. I am blessed to live in this time of advanced technology. I am amazed every time I visit with my son, daughter-in-law, and grandchildren in Australia by way of Skype.

January 18. I have been blessed for the past forty-two years to have the best medical office staff in America. They are hard-working, loyal to the nth degree, competent, and bright. They are friendly, meet the public well and relate to them as family. They are cross-trained and help each other without being told when one falls behind. They are my friends and promote our practice in the community. I can't say enough or praise them enough. I love them all.

January 19. I am blessed with a close and caring family.

January 20. It is a blessing to have friends who grieve with you in times of sorrow. No words of wisdom are necessary; just simply being present, hugging, and sharing tears.

January 21. I am blessed with good neighbors.

January 22. I was blessed to be born after the Depression, to be a teenager in the '50s, which psychologists say was the best time in history to raise teenagers, and blessed to have practiced medicine in the "Golden Era of Medicine" when it was profitable and before government controlled medicine took control. Regrettably, bureaucratic control has taken a lot of fun and satisfaction out of the practice of medicine and greatly affected the quality of medicine practiced.

January 23. I am blessed with three fine sons who are all exceptional and accomplished, raising good families and contributing to society. Bryan, the oldest, is a Harvard-trained psychiatrist who is a professor at Drexel Medical in Philadelphia, heading up the residency training program. Jim (our middle child), a lawyer who, after a head injury, turned artist and researcher, and is finishing his PhD at the University of Melbourne in Australia doing pioneering research in how epilepsy affects artistic creativity, presenting his research to international forums. Brad's first love is raising Hereford cattle, but he also has a very successful mortgage company.

January 24. I am thankful to be an adopted son of God, joint heir with Jesus Christ and destined to spend eternity with Him.

January 25. I am blessed with friends who pray for me.

January 26. I am blessed to belong to a family who believes in hugging, which is very curative.

January 27. I am blessed with a very loyal wife who puts my needs above her own.

January 28. I am blessed that I enjoy music from country to classic, especially gospel. We attend Gaither concerts often and listen to their CDs every night. We had the privilege of going on a Gaither cruise to Alaska.

January 29. I am blessed with nine grandchildren who are active, bright, full of life and laughter, and full of energy; they love their grandparents.

January 30. I am blessed to have a love for and participate in sports, now as a spectator, but once very actively. It is a pleasure now watching the grandchildren and my favorite teams. Go Big Blue!

January 31. It is a blessing to be loyal to my friends, family, church, schools, universities, and various organizations and feel a reciprocal loyalty from them.

February 1. I am blessed to work at a profession I enjoy.

February 2. I am blessed to live in the day and time of rapid transfer of information by cell phone, e-mail, 24-hour cable television news, iPads, etc.

February 3. I am thankful for spring, summer, and fall. Winter is tolerated for Christmas and basketball.

February 4. I am thankful for flowers that add so much beauty and happiness to life.

February 5. I am thankful for science and all the people who have added to my comfort, health and satisfaction, and appreciation of life by their dedicated contributions of invention and discovery, often through an entire lifetime of work.

February 6. I am thankful for our founding fathers who gave us the Declaration of Independence, the Constitution, the Bill of Rights, and Constitutional amendments.

February 7. I am thankful for those serving in our armed forces and for all the hundreds of thousands who paid the supreme sacrifice for the liberty we enjoy. I learned long ago that freedom is not free but is paid for with blood and treasure.

February 8. I am blessed to have had a mother who prayed for me on her knees by the sofa every night.

February 9. I am blessed to realize that God lives in my heart in the form of the Holy Spirit, who cleans up our inside to the degree that we will let Him, and this transformation is expressed externally by the Fruits of the Spirit which the Apostle Paul in Galatians lists as 1) love, 2) joy, 3) peace, 4) patience, 5) kindness, 6) goodness, 7) faithfulness, 8) gentleness, and 9) self-control.

February 10. I am blessed with friends who check on me and ask how I'm doing and wish me the best.

February 11. I am thankful that nothing can separate me from the love of God, and no one can take me out of Jesus' hands.

February 12. I'm thankful for our local hospital, where good medicine is practiced and patients are transferred to the right tertiary hospital at the right time, by the proper transportation system. We now even have helicopter service.

February 13. I am thankful for parents who taught us about priorities in life.

February 14. I have been blessed with good health and did not miss a complete day of work until the age of sixty-two and very few since.

February 15. I am thankful for America's unequaled prosperity in my lifetime and pray that we can come to our senses about debt reduction in our present economy.

February 16. I am blessed to belong to a Christ-centered church.

February 17. I am thankful for my gardening ability and God's good earth. On this cold day I'm anxious to see the flowers come out again.

February 18. On this day I have been blessed to witness the funeral celebration of Whitney Houston, one of America's most famous music icons. Love and forgiveness were supreme and not one reference was made to hate or racial prejudice. It was one of the most moving events I have witnessed in years and all four hours were covered by Fox News. Love was the theme, and the sermon Christ-centered and evangelical. Imagine that!

February 19. I am thankful for laughter, which is contagious and healing. It is the universal language.

February 20. I am thankful for Penny Frank, who is our children's director at church. She effectively gets across a point in each children's sermon that the children will never forget. It helps me, too!

February 21. I have been blessed and am thankful for the opportunity to travel in the USA and around the world, enjoying God's beautiful creations.

February 22. I am thankful for the interstate highway system, which is one of the marvels of the 20th century.

February 23. I am blessed to have had a good father who set a good example for me, who taught me to work hard and always do my best.

February 24. I have always been blessed to have a lot of friends who believe in me and trust me.

February 25. I am grateful to have always had a lot of infants and children around me. Every time I hold a baby, it makes me want to work harder to make this a better world for him/her to grow up in.

February 26. I am blessed to have a mother who taught me that Breckinridge County has enough "hurting people" to keep us all busy day and night. Also, she often said, "Don't neglect or forget to stop and smell the roses."

February 27. I am blessed to have been taught the principle that "in as much as ye have done it unto one of the least of these, my brethren, ye have done it unto me."

February 28. I am thankful to have enough food to eat, especially ice cream.

February 29. I am thankful for Leap Year – one extra day to enjoy life.

March 1. I am grateful for all the wonder drugs we have today.

March 2. I am thankful for each and every person who has had a positive influence on my life and contributed to my success.

March 3. I am thankful for all those who have forgiven me.

March 4. I am grateful for all those who have entrusted me with their medical care.

March 5. My life has been blessed by basketball.

March 6. I have been blessed with the vision of hope.

March 7. I am thankful I have been taught the way to happiness. This is one of the few poems I've ever written:

> To love and be loved,
> To be content with what you have and what you do,
> To accept yourself as you are and others as they are,
> To do what you think God wants you to do,
> This is the way to happiness.

March 8. I am thankful I don't have to attend our church business meetings more than once a month.

March 9. I am blessed to have many sharing friends.

March 10. I am blessed to have a clear mind.

March 11. I am blessed to have been raised in a two-parent family with eight siblings, with all the things you learn from a large family.

March 12. I feel blessed by God's faithful love.

March 13. It is a blessing to be called "Grandad."

March 14. I am thankful for riding lawnmowers.

March 15. I am blessed to have medical patients who take time to thank me for my services.

March 16. It is a blessing to have a Bible, which is God's Word--"a light unto my feet and a lamp unto my path."

March 17. I am thankful for all of God's promises, especially the promise that I will be a joint heir with Christ and that I will know all things. No more Googling!

March 18. I am grateful for pets. I have had some favorites and observe the companionship they provide for so many folks.

March 19. I am thankful for our new church facility, which is beautiful and functional, enhancing our worship and multiplying our programs and service to the community.

March 20. I am thankful for the recording of history and what the past teaches us about the present – preparing us to deal with the future.

March 21. I am thankful for the Gaithers, the lyrics they write, and the beautiful way they put them to music.

March 22. I am thankful for all the conservative leaders in America.

March 23. I am grateful for all the evangelical missionaries around the world, risking their lives to take the gospel to all nations.

March 24. I am thankful for all those people, both Christian and secular, who volunteer their time for all the service organizations in our community, country, and around the world.

March 25. I am thankful for God's plan of salvation.

March 26. I am thankful for America's charitable attitude.

March 27. I am thankful that God is in control.

March 28. I am thankful that most children are wanted and have parents who accept their responsibilities.

March 29. Where I vacation in the Smokey Mountains, I am blessed with beautiful sunsets. They always make me think of our second son, Jim, who gets the biggest thrill out of sunsets.

March 30. I am blessed because Jesus died on the cross to pay for my sins.

March 31. I am blessed with a faithful, loving wife.

April 1. I am blessed to have the resources to help people in need.

April 2. I am thankful we have the finest medical care in the world and for all my physician friends who have given me personally their best skills and attention.

April 3. I am thankful for fruit, which is delicious, nutritious, and attractive to the eye.

April 4. I am grateful for research, which enriches all our lives. Entrepreneurship is the foundation of most research.

April 5. I was blessed with the greatest mother-in-law in the world. I told her this often.

April 6. I am blessed to be able to work in the church woods and walking track. I love nature, and it makes me feel closer to God.

April 7. I am blessed to have a wife who is an excellent cook and in addition is attentive to my nutrition.

April 8. I am blessed to have three sons who like to talk to their dad and share their problems and achievements.

April 9. This is my mother's birthday. I don't think anyone ever had a better mother. If I didn't want to talk, which was often, she would honor my silence. If I wanted to talk, she would listen for as long as I wanted to talk or vent. Her suggestions would be ever so subtle, but never critical.

April 10. More about Mom! She taught me how to be an encourager. She had what I call a "note ministry." Every morning after the breakfast dishes were done, she would sit at the kitchen table and write 4-6 notes of encouragement to those in the community she thought needed it the most. I have had patients show me notes they had kept for more than fifty years, with comments that it was Mom who helped them get through bad times. This was a woman who had eleven children, seven of them in the middle of the Great Depression of the '30s

April 11. I am blessed that many people pray for me.

April 12. I am blessed with all God's promises in the Bible.

April 13. I am blessed with an abundance of beautiful flowers in our yard.

April 14. I am thankful for all those who have courage to take a stand.

April 15. I am blessed to have many dedicated physicians to take care of me and to refer my patients to.

April 16. Vacations and travel are a blessing.

April 17. I am thankful for all the special blessings and talents God gave me and you.

April 18. I am thankful for many years of good health and an exceptional amount of energy.

April 19. I am thankful for good winners and good losers. I love to hear athletes give credit for their success to God.

April 20. I am blessed I understand the statement "Loving God and loving each other."

April 21. I am blessed to be free of cancer. I observe its devastation daily.

April 22. I am blessed to have friends who love me enough to tell me when I'm wrong.

April 23. I am blessed to have a sound mind and common sense.

April 24. I am blessed to have a wife who forgives me.

April 25. I am blessed to be associated with some of the finest Christians in the world who effortlessly demonstrate "the Fruits of the Spirit."

April 26. I am blessed that the majority of my patients trust me, love me, and respect me.

April 27. I am blessed that my wife doesn't require me to shop with her.

April 28. I am thankful to live in the most generous country in the world.

April 29. I am blessed to be free to worship at the Hardinsburg Baptist Church in freedom and truth with no persecution to date. I am thankful for my French Huguenot ancestors who survived persecution and escaped to the United States in 1617.

April 30. I am blessed to be a good sleeper.

May 1. People with musical talent are a blessing to me.

May 2. People who share are a particular blessing to me.

May 3. God's creation is a blessing to me.

May 4. I am thankful for air conditioning. It is truly a blessing.

May 5. I am thankful and grateful for all veterans of war who sacrificed their lives or put their lives in danger for our freedom.

May 6. I am thankful for those who are loyal.

May 7. I am thankful for Google. I have never tried to get an answer to a question and failed. It's amazing!

May 8. I am thankful for people who help others in their hour of greatest need.

May 9. I am blessed to be conscious of cleanliness.

May 10. I am blessed to be a part of God's creation.

May 11. I am thankful that in Kentucky we have an abundance of water which is clean, sterile, and fluoridated, which amazingly prevents cavities in our children's teeth.

May 12. I am thankful for the Bible, God's word for us to live by. I have also been blessed to be a part of the Gideon Ministry.

May 13. I am blessed to be a member of the family of God, "joint heir with Jesus Christ."

May 14. I am thankful for all our remarkable pharmaceuticals.

May 15. I am blessed to live in a house with a beautiful yard with flowers, shrubs, rabbits, squirrels, and many, many species of birds that we feed.

May 16. I am blessed with a family who likes sports as much as I do. Clint made the All-Star Team in baseball while being the smallest player on the team and perhaps the league. He says, "I'm trying to grow. I'm just not good at it."

May 17. I am thankful for seat belts, air bags, and all the newer automobile safety devices.

May 18. I am thankful for wide-screen HD televisions which make viewing more enjoyable, especially sports.

May 19. I am thankful for 24-hour cable news, especially Fox News.

May 20. I am blessed to have been disciplined as a child – with love.

May 21. I am blessed that we can all enjoy the wonders of nature.

May 22. I am blessed with a large garden that provides vegetables for family and friends all summer.

May 23. I am blessed with the privilege to work.

May 24. I am blessed to live in a country built by the free enterprise system.

May 25. I am blessed with grandchildren's smiles when they see me.

May 26. I am blessed with Sunday worship and rest.

May 27. I am blessed with a love for books.

May 28. I am blessed with modern farming machinery that takes the back-breaking work out of farming.

May 29. I am blessed with the freedom to debate issues and vote for my position.

May 30. I am blessed to have had exceptional Sunday School teachers down through the years.

May 31. As a Christian, I am blessed to be indwelled by the Holy Spirit that leads me to develop in my life the "Fruits of the Spirit" – love, joy, peace, patience, kindness, goodness, faithfulness, gentleness, and self-control. The Holy Spirit is patient with us and lets us develop at a pace we allow. I'm not finished yet!

June 1. I am blessed with the ability to go to sleep quickly and sleep well.

June 2. I am blessed to be a forgiving person. My wife calls it a "poor memory."

June 3. Christ forgives and forgets our sins, so my past is taken care of. Jesus says, "I am come that they might have life and that they might have it more abundantly." So my present is taken care of. Those of us who believe in Jesus Christ will "have eternal life." So my future is taken care of. "I do not know what the future holds, but I know who holds the future." What a blessing!

June 4. It's a blessing to observe God's creatures. A pair of birds we call Kill Dees built a nest in a flower bed 10 feet from our house near the pool. We had to take care of the pool so we co-existed with the birds for 6-8 weeks. Eventually the eggs hatched, and within a few days the family departed. They taught us a lot about family responsibility. Of note was the monogamous relationship and contribution of each of the pair.

June 5. Good intentions carried out are a blessing. Here is one of my favorite poems by Dr. Charles Jarvis.

> *Life's a trial and life's a worry.*
> *Life's a problem, life's a hurry.*
> *Life's a busy crowded way,*
> *Good intentions gone astray.*
>
> *I had a friend the other day*
> *I haven't now 'cause he passed away.*
> *I meant to write, to phone, to call*
> *But he didn't hear from me at all.*
>
> *I only hope he now can see*
> *What his friendship meant to me.*
> *Life's a busy crowded way.*
> *Good intentions gone astray.*

(This makes me thankful for Mom's note ministry.)

June 6. I am thankful for the variety of the seasons.

June 7. It is a blessing to have a Christ-centered pastor in a Christ-centered church who preaches the Word as presented in the Bible. Brother Doug Miller has the courage to address moral and social issues as presented in the Bible.

June 8. Random acts of kindness are a blessing for the giver and receiver.

June 9. I am thankful for rain and snow. Being raised on a farm we are made aware of the importance of rain. Farmers say, "It always rains a day before it's too late." That gives us hope. As for snow, I can settle for a white Christmas, but I admit some of the most beautiful scenes of nature I've ever seen involve snow.

June 10. It is a blessing to feel forgiven. Being unrepentant separates us from God. It's a blessing to be forgiven by a spouse, family member, friend, or your worst enemy. Also, when you mature, you discover that it's a blessing and it gives you a good feeling to forgive someone else.

June 11. We can get a blessing out of hard times. God uses trials and pain to grow our character. Trials will happen – we will have pain. God is often found in the heart of the storm, not outside it.

June 12. A close church family is a blessing.

June 13. Today is my 53rd anniversary. It is a blessing to have a stable marriage and a loving and devoted wife.

June 14. I am thankful for the University of Kentucky basketball. Who else other than a "Big Blue" fan would be keeping up with basketball in June? It takes hard work twelve months a year to get the top recruiting class in America four years in a row and the potential for six years in a row in the making.

June 15. I'm thankful for hot weather. I'm cold-natured and freeze in the winter.

June 16. I'm thankful for our children's program at church. Children's sermons are my favorite.

June 17. I am thankful for e-mail and Skype, which keeps me in touch with my children within reach of the keyboard.

June 18. I am blessed with improving health.

June 19. I am thankful that our new church facility improves the quality and joy of worship.

June 20. I am blessed to belong to a family that has family reunions. They are fun and keep a family knitted solidly together. My mother was a great advocate of family reunions.

June 21. I am grateful for the scholarships that helped me get my education. I appreciate all those who contributed to those scholarships.

June 22. I am thankful for vegetables. We live out of our garden all season with the finest food the earth can produce.

June 23. There are many encouragers in our church, for which I am grateful.

June 24. I am thankful again for generous and thoughtful friends. They are more precious than any worldly possession.

June 25. I was blessed to be raised up in a home that provided a lot of security. We didn't have much, but we didn't know it mattered.

June 26. I was blessed to have been raised to root for the underdog. I was always sympathetic with the kid who got chosen last and would choose them near the first to make them happy. Recently a handicapped man I was in grade school with told my nurse that I treated him better than anyone in my class. I would imagine that is why grades 6 through 12 they elected me president of our class. I have continued to root for the underdog.

June 27. I am blessed to have had a mother who taught us to have a servant's attitude.

June 28. I was also taught by my parents to never forget where you came from and to "grow where you are planted."

June 29. I am blessed to have been taught by my parents to take a stand and speak out when necessary or appropriate.

June 30. I am blessed to have learned early on that being a husband and father is more important than being a physician.

July 1. I have been blessed to have been taught by my mother to have an attitude of gratitude.

July 2. I have been blessed to have been taught not to be prejudiced toward race, color, creed, social standing, or economic status. We are all God's children. We believers are His adopted children.

July 3. Indoor plumbing and bathrooms are a blessing. We didn't have these when I was a child.

July 4. I am blessed to be an American and realize again today that we stand on the shoulders of our ancestors who fought, died, and gave up their blood and treasure for our independence. Fireworks are a nice reminder.

July 5. It is a blessing to see good, ordinary, non-political folks come together in America to address our critical problems of national debt, too-big government, too- stringent regulations, and too much opposition to the free enterprise system which made America great. The loss of it threatens the security of our children and grandchildren.

July 6. A friend came by today to see how we are doing. What a blessing.

July 7. It has been a blessing to be involved in building a half-mile walking track around our beautiful wooded church property. I put up a sign that says "While you walk, think about God." The scenery changes from woods to beautiful cropland to beautiful pastures filled with cattle and back to woods. Why should we think about God? Because He wants us to. Sometimes we just need to be worshipful, sometimes we need comforting, sometimes we need repentance and forgiveness, sometimes we simply need fellowship, and at all times we need to give thanks.

July 8. It is also a blessing to build a soccer field next to our new church. We are involved in Upward Soccer, which is good for the children, parents, and grandparents. It introduces many of the children to Jesus for the first time and provides badly needed exercise. We also built a gym for Upward Basketball.

July 9. I am blessed to live in a country where we have freedom of speech where I can speak out against same-sex marriage and give my money for the pro-life movement and other conservative causes.

July 10. Babies of all species are a blessing, from our own, to puppies, to wild animals. I once was at the nursing home and glanced into a room and there an elderly lady was lying on her back in bed with the most beautiful satisfying smile on her face. I went in to see why and found she had two little puppies - one under each arm. She was participating in the nursing home's "puppy therapy." That's the way babies affect me.

July 11. What a blessing to watch the baptism of my grandsons, one of them by their father, which is allowed and encouraged at the Severns Valley Baptist Church.

July 12. I am blessed to know a lot of good common folk who are good neighbors and treat you right. You can count on them. They do right simply because it is right!

July 13. It is a blessing to have a banker who will help you in all circumstances.

July 14. Strawberries are a blessing.

July 15. It is a blessing to have people pray for you.

July 16. Many of the things that influence my life now I learned in Sunday School and Bible School and are profound blessings. I still learn from the "Children's Sermons," my favorite part of the Sunday morning service.

July 17. As a physician, I am blessed with other physicians in my life who have helped me, influenced me, encouraged me, and set a good example for me. They are a definite blessing in my life.

July 18. My life has been blessed by the Old Testament patriarchs and prophets, the apostles of the New Testament, and the example and commandments of Jesus Christ. They have indeed been a blessing.

July 19. I have been blessed with a positive attitude. Life has its troubles, but my mother said often, "This, too, shall pass."

July 20. It seems like most of the troubles in my life have piled up toward the end. It is a blessing to remember that Job of the Old Testament remained true to God and was eventually doubly blessed. Our faith should not depend on the current circumstances.

July 21. My New Year's resolution to count my blessings and name one every day has indeed been a blessing.

July 22. I may be repetitive, but it is a blessing to know Jesus Christ as my personal Lord and Savior.

July 23. Fellowship with fellow Christians is a blessing. We built a pavilion in the woods on the church property and have frequent ice cream suppers, wiener roasts, and bring our favorite spreads there.

July 24. Our cabin in the Smokey Mountains is a blessing. The Smokies are one of God's most beautiful creations.

July 25. Summer is a blessing to me. I like everything about it.

July 26. I know a man who demonstrates all the Fruits of the Spirit; namely, love, peace, joy, patience, kindness, goodness, faith, gentleness, and self-control. He is a blessing to me.

July 27. Photography is a blessing. I am surrounded by hundreds of photos of my children and grandchildren. I have over 11,000 on my computer. What a blessing to receive a new photo by e-mail. It's often the "lift of the day."

July 28. Technologically skilled workers are a blessing. Our educational system should not release any student until they have acquired a skill that will earn them a livelihood. We need more vocational training and fewer college graduates.

July 29. Chemistry is a blessing. From petroleum alone, we enjoy thousands of products that make our lives better.

July 30. It is a blessing to know people of great faith. The Bible says you can't please God without faith. Abraham of the Old Testament was a man of great faith. In Hebrews Chapter 11, he heads up God's Honor Roll of Faith. That is one honor roll we should strive to make.

July 31. It is a blessing we have people who are willing to adopt unwanted children. Calvin and Lori's baby was born today, and what a blessing for that baby to have them for his parents.

August 1. We have just lived through the hottest and driest July since 1956. It is a blessing to know we will survive and cool days and rain will come again. How's that for faith?

August 2. It's a blessing to know we have a sovereign God. I believe it's not what happens to us, it's how we react to what happens to us that counts. God is in control. We are incapable of understanding everything that happens, but we can accept that there is a reason for everything that happens, both good and bad.

August 3. Life is a blessing. It is precious and should be respected, cherished, and honored. It should be protected, from the unborn to the geriatric. It should be loved and enjoyed every day. It is a gift from God.

August 4. God's grace is a blessing, giving us what we don't deserve. "How can I thank You enough for all the things You have done for me?"

August 5. Those who show tenderness and gentleness are a blessing.

August 6. God's love is a blessing. God is love, the very essence of love. You can count on it.

August 7. It was a blessing seeing our second grandson baptized, knowing I will spend eternity with him. Our prayers are that all the grandchildren will accept Jesus as their personal Lord and Savior.

August 8. It is a blessing that adoption is available for those couples unable to have a baby. The Bohanans got a newborn baby boy this week, and their excitement was a joy to behold. It is also a blessing that there are unwed women who will carry their unwanted pregnancies to term and give their babies a good adopted home and future.

August 9. It is a blessing to know that you can't do anything or say anything that will keep God from loving you.

August 10. A day of rest on Sunday is a decided blessing.

August 11. Watching the Olympic athletes perform and hearing many of them give God the glory for their talents and gifts is a blessing.

August 12. Miracles are a blessing. As a physician, I witness them every day.

August 13. Hearing fellow Christians give their testimonies is a definite blessing.

August 14. It is a blessing to see people stand on their principles, like the owner of Chick-Fil-A. It was also a blessing to see the hundreds of thousands of people who gave their support to his stand.

August 15. It is a blessing to worship with the family of God.

August 16. It is a blessing to have sons who will call and ask for advice.

August 17. It is a blessing to tithe when you give with joy in your heart and give God credit for everything in your life.

August 18. It is a blessing to watch your grandchildren on Skype and among their first words learned are "Grammy" and "Grandad," said with a big smile on their faces.

August 19. When life is going bad or when you are discouraged, it's a blessing to know God is on your side.

August 20. It is a blessing that those with gifts of musical talents share their gifts with the rest of us.

August 21. The elderly among us are a blessing and a treat and the source of tremendous wisdom.

August 22. Fellow Christians who encourage us are a blessing.

August 23. Answered prayers are a blessing – including those answered "yes," those answered "no" and those answered "wait a while." We should accept God's wisdom.

August 24. The ancient art of the practice of medicine combined with the modern technology of medicine is indeed a blessing.

August 25. Modern transportation is a blessing.

August 26. The computer is a mixed blessing.

August 27. School starting again is a blessing for all.

August 28. Quietness is a blessing. "Be still and know that I am God."

August 29. It is a blessing to live in a country that is governed by the Rule of Law.

August 30. The opportunity of entrepreneurship in America is a blessing.

August 31. To live out the American Dream is a blessing for us and a challenge to pass on to our children and grandchildren.

September 1. Those who made the supreme sacrifice for the freedom of our country are a blessing.

September 2. After forty-eight years of practicing medicine, I have given myself a day off. That is definitely a blessing.

September 3. Every functioning part of our bodies is a blessing that we never think about until it malfunctions.

September 4. It is a blessing to have an outstanding secretary.

September 5. Grandmothers are a blessing, especially my "Grandma." I have great memories of her personality and her strong character.

September 6. It is a blessing to know people who do what they say they are going to do and you can count on it.

September 7. Funerals that celebrate life are a blessing.

September 8. Life is a blessing – every second of it. "The precious present!"

September 9. Vaccines are a blessing to humanity.

September 10. Loving your neighbor as yourself is a blessing to both parties.

September 11. Curiosity is a blessing. Nosiness it not! My oldest son must have asked me a gazillion questions while he was growing up. He became valedictorian, magna cum laude, Phi Beta Kappa and a medical school professor.

September 12. The 24-hour news cycle is a mixed blessing.

September 13. Appreciative family, friends, and employees are a blessing.

September 14. It's a blessing to have a wife who won't stay mad at you for more than 24 hours.

September 15. It is a blessing to know that into this life some rain must fall. Remember my mother's philosophy, "This, too, shall pass."

September 16. What a blessing it is to have a job where I work for the patient. The worst thing that has happened in my career is the government coming between me and my patients. Obamacare, if not repealed, will finish destroying medical care as we have always known it.

September 17. Being a member of Gideons International is a blessing knowing that a Bible you helped purchase and distribute around the world was responsible for presenting God's plan of salvation to someone maybe on the other side of the globe.

September 18. It is a blessing to have a love of history, because it helps us avoid repeating errors of the past.

September 19. Freedom is a gift of God and one of our greatest blessings.

September 20. It is a thrill and blessing to see young people profess faith in Jesus Christ, and those in the church who disciple them are an equal blessing.

September 21. Bumper stickers and church readerboards often carry messages that bless me.

September 22. Hard times are a blessing often disguised. I've learned that many times from experience.

September 23. The excitement of the creative minds of my nine grandchildren is a unique blessing.

September 24. Receiving various cards, especially Thank You cards, is a blessing.

September 25. Recognition for the large and small things you do in life is a blessing.

September 26. Sharing your garden with your neighbors and friends is a blessing.

September 27. Keeping your bills paid is a blessing.

September 28. Knowing someone is praying for you is a blessing. Once a hundred-year-old man, a godly man in the hospital, said,

"Dr. Chambliss, I pray for you every night." My mother prayed for me on her knees every night as long as she lived. My wife prays for me daily. With these three praying for me, how can I go wrong?

September 29. Noon naps are a blessing.

September 30. Family reunions at Disney World, Great Smokey Mountains, and others are a blessing.

October 1. Death often is a blessing.

October 2. Precious memories are a blessing. How they linger!

October 3. Practicing medicine for forty-nine years has been a blessing.

October 4. I am blessed to have children who call home often.

October 5. I was blessed to have had a wonderful mother-in-law and father-in-law whose anniversary is today. They were the salt of the earth type people – the best.

October 6. It is a blessing to have a good sense of humor.

October 7. Children who pursue academic excellence are a blessing.

October 8. Children who respect you are a blessing.

October 9. A loyal, faithful, and loving wife who has put up with me for fifty-three years is a special blessing. We celebrate her birthday today.

October 10. Fall colors are a blessing.

October 11. It is a blessing to have been raised with discipline and love and to raise your children in the same way.

October 12. It is a blessing that we have service organizations, church organizations, and neighbors who take care of the needy. America has always been the most generous country in the world.

October 13. It is a blessing to be taught to strive to be humble and grateful.

October 14. It is a blessing to have a wife who shares the same values in religion and politics and love for University of Kentucky basketball.

October 15. It is a blessing to know that everything you throw out comes back to you. Just remember that it is not necessarily from the same person, but maybe two or three people removed.

October 16. It is a blessing to know that you have friends who will cover your backside.

October 17. It's a blessing to know that friends are a family you choose.

October 18. "Doctors have a front row seat to the entire panorama of human life," and that is a unique blessing.

October 19. It is a blessing to know that criticism is destructive and causes a downward spiraling of our spiritual life.

October 20. Good employees are a blessing.

October 21. Sunshine after a dreary day is a blessing.

October 22. People with a cheerful attitude are a blessing.

October 23. When things don't go our way, it is a blessing to remember that God is in control.

October 24. It is a blessing to know that we are our brother's keeper and practice it.

October 25. It is a blessing to know the joy of giving.

October 26. It is a blessing to have a friend for a physician.

October 27. My mother's motto has always been a blessing to me. "Good, better, best. Never let it rest until the best becomes better and the better becomes best!"

October 28. It is a blessing to have the opportunity to live a life of service.

October 29. Development and research are a blessing. Those involved make a great contribution to all our lives.

October 30. It is a blessing to witness the outpouring of food, supplies, free labor, and prayers from one part of the USA to another during a catastrophic hurricane, flood, or tornado. This puts FEMA to shame. Americans are generous people and should be relied on more than a centralized government.

October 31. It is a blessing being a child. My mother's philosophy was to let a child be a child – there is much time later to be an adult. She insisted on children having their play time.

November 1. It is a blessing to know a blessing when we see one.

November 2. Wealth is a blessing when properly used.

November 3. A peaceful home is a blessing.

November 4. Growth is a blessing and a key to happiness.

November 5. Good health is a blessing and should be something we thank God for daily.

November 6. Daily fellowship with God is a blessing and free for the asking. Along that same line, salvation is a blessing – free, but not cheap.

November 7. Having a Teflon personality is a blessing.

November 8. Often, having a bad memory is a blessing, especially forgetting all the petty things others do to us.

November 9. The ability to smile is a special blessing and should be cultivated. It is one of the major factors in our success and our ability to lead and influence others. It helps win friends and influence people favorably.

November 10. Competition and success are a blessing. Not keeping score and giving every child a trophy for participation is definitely not a blessing or helpful to that child.

November 11. Getting through adolescence without smoking, drinking, getting pregnant, or getting someone pregnant is a fortunate blessing. Getting your life off to a good start usually determines how it will end up.

November 12. It is a blessing to see a mother and father take care of a handicapped child for years with love and great sacrifice of their personal lives. Joe and Barbara Miller did such an outstanding job with Julie for fifteen years with tender care given with love. It thrilled me to see Julie respond to their love. In our society they are the true heroes--my heroes.

November 13. Being forgiven is a blessing in that it restores our fellowship with God.

November 14. Truth is a blessing because a knowledge of it sets you free.

November 15. My 91-year-old sister had a near fatal heart attack today. It was a blessing to see how calm she was in the face of death. Her response all her life to the question "How are you?" has been "I'm ok." She is right! Come what may, Christians are "ok."

November 16. I received this e-mail today from my oldest son. "Daddy, so sorry you had to go through this (Lillian's heart attack) as a brother and a doctor. It must have been hard to have had the life of your older sister in your hands. You have always been willing to take on the hard jobs, and we have always been able to count on you to accomplish them to the best that life makes possible. With respect and gratitude, Bryan." It is truly a blessing to have sons who treat you with respect and gratitude.

November 17. Bible study is a blessing, opening our minds to a greater understanding of God.

November 18. Freedom is a blessing, given to us by God and the sacrifice of our forefathers with their blood and treasure and guaranteed by the Constitution.

November 19. Good health is a blessing we seldom fully appreciate until we lose it.

November 20. Reconciliation is a blessing, and the reward is an unparalleled joy of life.

November 21. Insurance is a blessing we seldom appreciate until we receive the benefits.

November 22. It's a blessing to set aside one special day to thank God for all our blessings. Turkey is overrated. Eating Thanksgiving dinner with four grandsons is a special blessing.

November 23. It is a blessing to have someone love us.

November 24. Chocolate is a blessing – especially Ghirardelli dark chocolate – the one that sounds like a bacteria or a disease.

November 25. Church prayer groups are a blessing. We have an e-mail prayer alert in our church where prayer alerts go out to the entire membership who have internet. When my sister went into the cardiac cath lab after her heart attack, she was covered by the prayers of the church. This is just one example. We take turns at needing each other's prayers.

November 26. Failures are a blessing that have kept me humble.

November 27. I am thankful for friends who give me tickets to the University of Kentucky basketball games occasionally.

November 28. It is a blessing to live in America, a land so rich our worst struggles would be a paradise to inhabitants of most third-world countries and most socialist countries.

November 29. Rest is a blessing. Most of us need 7-8 hours of sleep and some need more. A rested body is more productive, and nothing makes us sleep better than a hard day's work.

November 30. The Christmas season again is a blessing. The "war on Christmas" starts again, and my wife and I will certainly let everyone know which side we are on including a lighted star and cross on top of the gazebo complete with a nativity scene. Christ coming to earth as God incarnate is the ultimate blessing. Study His life, and you will know what God is like.

December 1. We are blessed if we realize that "love is the theme."

December 2. Kindness is a blessing, and a kind word is the best therapy. I am blessed with a kind wife.

December 3. Laughter is a universal language and a blessing to all. It is also a major contributor to good health.

December 4. It is a blessing to know that God makes each day. "Rejoice and be happy in it."

December 5. It is a blessing to know that heaven will be my home.

December 6. It is a blessing to know that the remedy for sin is repentance.

December 7. It is a blessing that the body has such power to heal itself. Physicians often help and sometimes interfere, but most of the body's restorative power is built in by our Creator.

December 8. Speaking of healing, the Bible recommends intercessory prayer for improved results, and that is a blessing. Duke University School of Medicine has done a scientific double-blind study that proves it, and we need to take advantage of it.

December 9. It is a blessing that Christ is the center of Christmas. Of all the people who ever lived, He has definitely had the most influence on the world and history, so why shouldn't we honor the Prince of Peace? (personal peace)

December 10. It is a blessing that we have a few politicians who will vote right for the good of the country even at the risk of being voted out in the next term.

December 11. Freedom of speech is such a blessing. Let's hope it will never be taken away from us. It could happen even in America.

December 12. Strong, close-knit families are a blessing. I am a Baptist, but I have observed, at least in my community, the Catholic families excel in this regard. They also produce hard-working children. I admire that!

December 13. It is a blessing to understand that we have Christian witness. The saddest thing is when someone loses his or her witness.

December 14. The Living Christmas Tree, a Christmas musical put on by the Hardinsburg Baptist Church for the past twenty-four years, is truly a blessing. Each year I say, "The best one yet." Sometimes I attend all three presentations.

December 15. Eating out is a blessing, providing a variety of good food and a relief for Janet.

December 16. Having a father-son relationship with God is a blessing. He invites it. We benefit from it. I recommend you read Psalm 103 every year, especially at Thanksgiving. King David understood the relationship and the benefits.

December 17. Friends who say "You look good" or "You haven't aged a bit" or simply ask "How are you?" are a blessing.

December 18. It is a blessing to have a purpose in life and a passion for what you do. Unfortunately, most people are not happy with their present employment.

December 19. Birthdays are a blessing. Today I am seventy-five years old. I will receive many cards, notes, and congratulations, with all the good memories they invoke. It should be a day to look ahead and move on with the resolve of the poet, Robert Frost, (with miles and miles before I sleep).

December 20. It is a blessing to know that you have the potential to be as good as the best person you know and as bad as the worst person you know. In your heart and soul, Madonna is not too far from Mother Teresa. Take care!

December 21. It is a blessing to know that death is not terminal – it's transitional.

December 22. It's a blessing not to accept mediocrity.

December 23. It is a blessing to know that often we win when we forget to keep score.

December 24. Teaching is a blessing, because to teach is to learn.

December 25. To celebrate the birthday of our Savior is a blessing extraordinaire. Can you imagine being joint heirs with Him? Can you fathom "saved by grace"?

December 26. Christmas activities coming to an end is often a blessing.

December 27. Visiting granddaughters is Philadelphia is a blessing.

December 28. Youth is a blessing if you can survive it.

December 29. Byron Crawford reminded me of this blessing of life. "I've learned that deep inside of each of us are little boxes filled with fear and courage, meanness and kindness, love and hate, and that the best people know which boxes to keep open and which to keep closed."

December 30. It's a blessing to have been taught that "From he who has much, much is expected."

December 31. It is a blessing to know that inside my soul are 365 more blessings and that all of them come from God. Thank you, God, for another year!

Count your blessings,
Name them one by one;
Count your many blessings,
See what God has done!

CPSIA information can be obtained
at www.ICGtesting.com
Printed in the USA
LVHW07s1700200518
577747LV00003B/3/P